PENGUIN BOOKS

ARCHAIC EGYPT

Walter Bryan Emery, the Edwards Professor of Egyptology in the University of London, was born in 1903. After preliminary training at the Liverpool University Institute of Archaeology, he went to Egypt for the first time in 1923 as an assistant on the staff of the Egypt Exploration Society's expedition to Tell el Amarna. Since that time, with the exception of six years' service with the British Army during the Second World War and four years in the Diplomatic Service in Cairo, his career was entirely devoted to excavation and discovery in the Nile Valley. Between 1924 and 1928 he directed the Mond Expedition of the University of Liverpool at Luxor and Armant, and in 1929 he was appointed Director of the Archaeological Survey of Nubia of the Egyptian Government Service of Antiquities, with instructions to explore and excavate all ancient sites in Lower Nubia which would be flooded by the second raising of the Aswan Dam. During the course of this work he discovered the tombs of the Late Nubian kings. The completion of the excavation of the fortress at Buhen in 1964 ended his work in Nubia. In 1936, he began the excavation of the Archaic Necropolis at Sakkara, and in 1970 the discovery was announced of a mausoleum of the sacred cows, one of the most important finds in the annals of Egyptology. Professor Emery died in March 1971.

Archaic Egypt

WALTER B. EMERY

ILLUSTRATIONS BY THE AUTHOR

PENGUIN BOOKS

PENGUIN BOOKS

Published by the Penguin Group
Penguin Books Ltd, 27 Wrights Lane, London W8 5TZ, England
Viking Penguin, a division of Penguin Books USA Inc.
375 Hudson Street, New York, New York 10014, USA
Penguin Books Australia Ltd, Ringwood, Victoria, Australia
Penguin Books Canada Ltd, 2801 John Street, Markham, Ontario, Canada L3R 1B4
Penguin Books (NZ) Ltd, 182–190 Wairau Road, Auckland 10, New Zealand

Penguin Books Ltd, Registered Offices: Harmondsworth, Middlesex, England

First published in Pelican Books 1961
Reprinted in Penguin Books 1991
1 3 5 7 9 10 8 6 4 2

Printed in England by Clays Ltd, St Ives plc
Set in Monotype Baskerville

CONTENTS

CONTENTS

LIST OF PLATES

7

8

LIST OF TEXT FIGURES

EDITORIAL FOREWORD

NOT long after 3000 B.C. the shadowy outline of predynastic Egypt begins to assume a sharper definition. Then, for the first time, we are confronted by written records of the First and Second Dynasties and can trace in hieroglyphic form the names of Narmer, and of Menes, immortally famed as the founder of a united kingdom. The succession of these kings has been handed down in dynastic lists, some of great antiquity, others of the Hellenistic era, and they span a period of about five hundred years. It is excavation and the science of archaeology that have set the seal on their historical authenticity.

Precisely at this stage the author of this book, Professor W. B. Emery, is privileged to speak, for he himself in the course of two decades has dug out at Sakkara no less than ten tombs which enclosed the relics and remains of kings and a queen of the first two dynasties. The intricate plans of these rich and splendid tombs, which the author has drawn with an exceptional skill, provide a basis also for reconstructing the palatial as well as the domestic architecture of archaic Egypt. And it is intensely interesting to see how remarkably well the written evidence of an archaic document such as the Palermo stone is confirmed not only by the sound tradition of Manetho's history but also by the progressive circumstantial evidence of archaeology. It is true that many problems still have to be solved: we are not even certain which of the kings was in fact the authentic Menes, but the difficulties have been clearly and fairly put by the author.

Now we are about to enter on yet another archaeological era when, as we hope, the evidence of Carbon 14 dating will provide us with a chronological yardstick with which we should be able to define the related development of the archaic kingdoms situated within the Tigris-Euphrates valleys on the one hand, and the Nile on the other. Professor Emery has shown at what points these very different and far distant kingdoms begin to show signs of a common technological knowledge. Some relationship there was, and indeed we know that under the First and Second Dynasties the Egyptians were trading in the Levant, mining copper in Sinai, travelling to Byblos for timber from Lebanon and Amanus, and to Crete probably for wine and oil.

Perhaps the later chapters are as fascinating as any in the book, with their account of what Egypt had achieved technically before about 2700 B.C., and how far its inhabitants had gone towards shaping the character of Egyptian civilization which stands out as brilliantly individual as any in the ancient world.

It may perhaps astonish many to hear that we may confidently predict that Egyptian soil still conceals beneath it for future diggers as much again as has ever come out of it. At Sakkara itself there is every reason to believe that many important discoveries are yet to be made, and we may conclude by expressing the hope that Professor Emery may one day return there and continue the work which his Egyptian colleagues have so cordially sponsored.

M. E. L. MALLOWAN
(Professor of Western Asiatic Archaeology,
University of London)

PREFACE

To attempt a synthesis of archaic Egypt at this time is perhaps a little premature, for excavations now in progress are revealing new material which may modify, or indeed drastically alter, many things which are at present regarded as beyond dispute. A full description of the civilization of the Nile valley during the first two dynasties would require a volume many times the size of this book, and my readers must understand that they are asked to accept a work which can only be little more than an introduction to a vast subject.

This, then, is an attempt to present a general outline of our knowledge of Egypt at the dawn of its history as a civilized state, to which our modern world, directly and indirectly, owes so much.

I wish to express my gratitude to Professor M. E. L. Mallowan for many valuable suggestions which have resulted in the introduction of several improvements both in the wording of many passages in the text and in the inclusion of several features I had overlooked.

W. B. EMERY

University College London

INTRODUCTION

THE DISCOVERY OF THE ARCHAIC PERIOD

BEFORE 1895, our knowledge of Egypt's history did not extend back beyond the reign of the Pharaoh Senefru, first king of the Fourth Dynasty (2680 B.C.), and to the historian of that day even he was a somewhat shadowy figure. It is true that we had the records of the Classical writers giving long lists of kings with what was considered the more important events of their reigns. We also had Egyptian lists of the kings right back to the legendary Menes, the first monarch of the First Dynasty and the founder of united Egypt. But these records, both Classical and Egyptian, were too fragmentary to give the scholar any sure foundation for historical research, and indeed many authorities regarded these kings as largely mythological. Certainly no one had any conception of the highly civilized state which existed in the Nile valley hundreds of years before the Pyramid Age.

All this was changed within a few years by the pick of the excavator. The discoveries of Petrie at Abydos, de Morgan at Nagadeh, and Quibell at Hieraconpolis revealed monuments and objects of these early kings and pushed back the frontiers of human history for more than five hundred years.

But let us examine the historical material available to the Egyptologist before these discoveries were made. The old Egyptian records consist of five king lists. These are:

1. The 'Tablet of Abydos' inscribed on the walls of a corridor of the temple of Seti at Abydos, listing a series of the *nesu** names of seventy-six kings from Menes to Seti I.

2. The 'Tablet of Karnak', now in Paris, originally listed the *nesu* names of sixty-two kings from Menes to Thotmose III, but it

* The *nesu*, or fourth name of the royal titulary, is now read as 'King of Upper and Lower Egypt'. It was taken by the king on his accession to the throne (see page 107).

does not compare with the Abydos list in value, for it was largely based on tradition rather than on formal chronicles.

3. The 'Tablet of Sakkara', found in the tomb of the Royal Scribe Thunery and now in the Cairo Museum, lists the *nesu* names of forty-seven kings beginning with Merbapen (Enezib) and ending with Rameses II. Merbapen was the sixth king of the First Dynasty, and the reason for the omission of his five predecessors was probably because the Sakkara tablet represented the king list according to the records of Lower Egypt, which did not recognize their sovereignty. The Abydos and Karnak lists representing Upper Egypt of course recognized the earlier kings.

4. The Turin Papyrus, written in hieratic, presents a list of kings with the length of each reign in years, months, and days. Unlike the monumental lists of Abydos, Karnak, and Sakkara, it does not stop with unification and the First Dynasty, but goes back beyond mortal kings to the dynasties of the gods. Another difference from the monumental lists is that the papyrus divides the groups of kings into periods. Compiled apparently in the Nineteenth Dynasty, the papyrus was undoubtedly a temple document and it was from such documents that the classical writers compiled their histories.

Valuable as it is, the Turin Papyrus is a tragedy, for more than half its value has been lost by careless treatment. Originally in the possession of the king of Sardinia, it was sent to Turin in a box without packing and it arrived at its destination broken into innumerable fragments. For years, scholars have worked to fit together what remained, but even so, in its restored state, many important gaps occur and the order of some of the kings remains in consequence a matter of debate. Of the seventeen kings of the Archaic Period, only ten are definitely recognizable.

5. Finally we have the so-called Palermo Stone which, like the Turin Papyrus, represents another tragedy for archaeological research. Only five small fragments of a great stone slab, originally about 7 ft long and 2 ft high, are in our hands and no record remains which will give a clue to where these pieces were found. Although the slab has obviously been broken up into small fragments, it is quite possible – even probable – that many more pieces of this invaluable monument remain, if we only knew where to look. As it is, we are faced with the tantalizing knowledge that a record of the

name of every king of the Archaic Period existed, together with the number of years of his reign and the chief events which occurred during his occupation of the throne. And these records were compiled in the Fifth Dynasty only about 700 years after the Unification, so that the margin of error would in all probability be very small. The slab of black basalt was lightly inscribed with the annals of the first five dynasties and also the names of the kings of Upper and Lower Egypt who ruled the two separate kingdoms before the Unification. The largest fragment has for many years been part of the collection in the Museum at Palermo, hence its name; a second piece is kept in the Cairo Museum, while a very small fragment is preserved in the Petrie Collection at University College London. Much research has been devoted to this important monument, but the conclusions arrived at by various authorities are conflicting and no entirely satisfactory reconstruction even of its general design has been achieved. However, one fact appears fairly certain: the second and third registers record the annals of the eight kings of the First Dynasty and the fourth and fifth registers the nine kings of the Second Dynasty. By applying Manetho's chronology (see below) to the year spacing on both the Palermo and Cairo fragments, it has been found that the termination of the four registers would end evenly. It would thus appear that Manetho's chronology of the first two dynasties is substantially correct and that he had definite authority for dividing the groups of kings into dynasties. We can only hope that some day the excavator's pick will reveal more of this monument, which for the historian is indeed beyond price.

Of the Classical sources Herodotus was of limited value, for he trusted too much in the stories related to him by the dragomans who guided him in his travels in Egypt, apparently making no attempt to establish the historical truth of the information thus obtained. But the fragmentary extracts taken from the writings of Manetho by Josephus and by the Christian chronographers Africanus (A.D. 300) and Eusebius (A.D. 340) were of immense importance and formed the framework on which Egyptian history has been built.

Manetho, a native of Sebennytus in Lower Egypt, lived in

the third century B.C. during the reign of Ptolemy II, on whose behalf he wrote a history of his native country. He was well qualified to do this, for he was apparently a priest of Heliopolis, the centre of Egyptian learning, and in consequence he must have had easy access to ancient records preserved in the temples. Unfortunately, Manetho's history is lost and we only have the extracts quoted by later writers six hundred years after the author's death, with all the resultant corruption through successive copying. Manetho divided his list of kings into dynasties, with the name of the locality from which each family originated. Certainly, with regard to the first two dynasties, his statements appear to be correct and there is little doubt that his authorities were sound. The Egyptian historian writing in Greek naturally gave a Greek form to the names of the kings, and, although archaeological research has proved that the monarchs he enumerates existed, the question of individual identification remains obscure.

These then were the only sources of knowledge regarding the foundation of Egypt's Pharaonic history that were available to the Egyptologist at the end of the last century. Meagre indeed; it is not surprising that the period of the first two dynasties could be dealt with in eleven pages in the first edition of Petrie's history published in 1894.

Suddenly the mists of historical obscurity were cleared by a series of remarkable discoveries in excavations at Abydos, Hieraconpolis, and Nagadeh.

In 1894 Quibell, digging near Edfu on the site of Hieraconpolis, found evidence of the first known kings of Egypt, the immediate predecessors of the First Dynasty. These were Selk, 'the Scorpion', and Narmer, the most notable relics of whom were the inscribed ceremonial mace-head of the former and the famous slate palette of the latter, both historical documents of great value. Quibell also discovered relics of the two Second Dynasty kings Kha-sekhem and Kha-sekhemui.

In 1896 de Morgan, then Director of the Service of Antiquities, discovered at Nagadeh a gigantic tomb which, from
the objects found in it, was identified as the burial place of
Hor-aha, first king of the First Dynasty. However, later research has shown that it is more probable that it was the
sepulchre of Nithotep, Hor-aha's mother. Apart from the
value of the architectural information which this great structure yielded, the discovery was rich in objects, the most important of which was a small ivory label inscribed with the
name of Hor-aha in conjunction with the name Men, thus
perhaps identifying this king with Manetho's Menes.

The following year Amélineau, digging in an area at Abydos known as Um-el-Qu'ab, 'the Mother of Pots', found a
group of great pit graves which were at that time identified
as the tombs of many of the kings of the Archaic Period. Unfortunately, Amélineau had little or no archaeological training and his method of excavating this site, one of the most
important ever found in Egypt, became another tragedy of
Egyptology. Financed as he was by collectors, Amélineau's
whole attention was directed to the collection of *objets d'art*
and he neglected even the most rudimentary recording of the
progress of his work. It was even reported that duplicate stone
vessels were destroyed in order to enhance the value of those
preserved. It is probable that such reports were exaggerated,
but certainly destruction of irreplaceable evidence through
ignorance and neglect was widespread. Having continued his
work of devastation for four years, Amélineau finally relin-
quished his concession. Petrie immediately reopened the excavations and in two seasons of brilliant research rescued
every scrap of evidence that his predecessor had not completely obliterated. By his painstaking work, he was able to
trace the architectural development of the funerary structures and to identify their royal owners. From the mass of
disordered evidence, he established the order of succession of

the kings of the First Dynasty so soundly that with small modifications his reconstruction of the chronological position of each monarch still stands at the present day and is confirmed by discoveries made at Sakkara forty years later.

With these discoveries the story of Egyptian civilization was pushed back nearly 600 years, but after the first excitement the interest of scholars subsided and research concerning the period diminished. Further discoveries were made at Tarkhan by Petrie in 1913 and Quibell established the existence of large archaic tombs at North Sakkara in 1912; but strangely enough these discoveries were not followed up by others. It would appear that scholars were discouraged by the paucity of inscribed material and their comparative failure to solve the many puzzles of archaic writing. New and exciting finds were revealing the cemeteries and settlements of the predynastic inhabitants of the Nile valley. The study of these finds claimed the attention of the Egyptologist who specialized in research into Egyptian origins, to the exclusion of further progress in adding to our knowledge of the birth of Pharaonic civilization.

The lull continued until 1932 when Reisner, with a view to the preparation of his great work on the evolution of funerary architecture, asked Cecil Firth, then Chief Inspector of Antiquities, to turn his attention to the long-neglected archaic cemetery at North Sakkara where Quibell had excavated in 1912. Firth cleared two areas, but died before he could fully record the results of his work, and the writer received instructions from the Director-General of the Department of Antiquities to re-excavate the areas he cleared so that they might be published. Firth's excavations had not been very detailed; the re-examination of part of a large First Dynasty tomb partly cleared by him resulted in some startling discoveries, and arrangements were made for the systematic clearance of the whole area. From 1936 to the outbreak of war this detailed work continued and a series of large tombs, almost certainly the northern counterparts of the royal monuments of the First Dynasty kings at Abydos, was discovered.

The work of excavation was renewed after the war and until 1956 was conducted by the writer for the Egypt Exploration Society on behalf of the Antiquities Service of the Egyptian Government. In addition to this, Zaki Saad, who assisted in the work at Sakkara before the war, has been engaged since 1942 in clearing a vast cemetery of the lesser nobility and the middle class of the First Dynasty which he discovered at Helwan on the east bank of the Nile opposite Sakkara. The excavation of these two great cemeteries which housed the dead of ancient Memphis 3000 years before Christ has yielded a new mass of material, and Egyptology has taken renewed interest in the problem of the origins of Pharaonic civilization.

Although much new inscribed material has been recovered, the certain interpretation of the archaic inscriptions yet escapes us; but progress is being made and, as more texts become available, there is little doubt that the philologist will finally discover the key which will open this valuable storehouse which contains the secret of the beginnings of Egypt's history. Already our knowledge of the architecture, art, epigraphy, pottery, stone vessels, and other materials is such that we can date these relics to the early, middle, and late parts of the First and Second Dynasties. Egypt's first Pharaohs are no longer shadowy figures of myth and legend, but with the advance in research are rapidly becoming real persons; the results of their achievements are often better defined and clearer to us than those of later periods.

But even with the increase of our knowledge concerning this remote period of Egypt's history, there still remain many features on which Egyptologists are not in agreement and in the various works dealing with the subject the student is often confused by the conflicting viewpoints of authorities who only too often fail to present the evidence for and against their conclusions. This is unfortunate but understandable, for on many facets of the history and culture of the period the evidence is so scanty that the full presentation of all the conflicting interpretations of one's colleagues would be impossible. This is so particularly in the case of the present work. Lack of space prevents me from giving all the evidence in support or otherwise of certain historical conclusions, or even of attempting the proper justification of opinions that may differ from those of other scholars. However, I think it would be appropriate here to summarize some of the more important points of difference.

First and most important is the vexed question of chronology. The diversity of opinion among Egyptian historians will be appreciated by an examination of the dating of the duration of the First and Second Dynasties submitted in the following selection of comparatively recent works:

BREASTED, *A History of Egypt*, 1921.   3400–2980 B.C. = 420 years.

HALL, *Cambridge Ancient History*, vol.   3500–3190 B.C. = 310   „
I, 1924.

WEIGALL, *A History of the Pharaohs*,   3407–2888 B.C. = 519   „
1925.

DRIOTON and VANDIER, *Les Peuples*   3197–2778 B.C. = 419   „
de l' Oriént Mediterranéen: l'Égypte,
1938.

SEWELL, *The Legacy of Egypt*, 1942.   3188–2815 B.C. = 373   „

FRANKFORT, *Kingship and the Gods*,   3100–2700 B.C. = 400   „
1948.

HAYES, *The Scepter of Ancient Egypt*,   3200–2780 B.C. = 420   „
1953.

The dating of the earlier Egyptologists, placing the foundation of united Egypt in the region of 4400 B.C., has long been discarded, and indeed the limited tests of that new aid to archaeological research – radiocarbon technique – have shown that a chronology based on the premise of a third complete Sothic cycle is certainly incorrect.* Nevertheless, as will be seen above, there is still considerable divergence among contemporary historians, and, with the exception of Weigall, no acceptance of Manetho's figure of about 550 years covering the period from the accession of Menes to the end of the Second Dynasty. Yet such a period would not seem excessive, from the archaeological evidence. At Sakkara it is certain that the great tombs of the early First Dynasty were in complete ruin by the end of the Second Dynasty. Structures that stood at least six metres in height were reduced to not more than one metre above their original ground level, and tombs of the early Third Dynasty were built on top of what remained of them. Such destruction of buildings of immense size and strength, with main walls varying from two to five metres in width, could only happen over a considerable period of time, and 550 years would in my view be a reasonable time to account for it. It is true that there is reason to doubt the strict accuracy of Manetho's figures, for they show every sign of being distorted by the carelessness of his copyists. Taking the First Dynasty as an example:

	Africanus	Eusebius (Armenian version)	Eusebius (from Syncellus)
Menes	62	30	60
Athothis	57	27	27
Kenkenes	31	39	39
Uenephes	23	42	42
Usaphaidos	20	20	20
Miebidos	26	26	26
Semempses	18	18	18
Bieneches	26	26	26
Total	253	252	252
	(actual 263)	(actual 228)	(actual 258)

*Dates obtained by radiocarbon technique in 1950, on wood from a roofing beam of Tomb 3035 at Sakkara, were as follows:

Total years 4803 ± 260 = between 3112 and 2592 B.C.

4961 ± 240 = between 3250 and 2770 B.C.

Moreover, one unmistakable error is revealed by the Cairo fragment of the Palermo Stone, for on it we have the reign of Semempses (Semerkhet) given as nine years, whereas Manetho, in all versions, gives it as eighteen years. But, as I have pointed out on page 23, Manetho's figures accord well with the year spacing on the Palermo Stone and, even with the variations of the duration of individual reigns submitted by his copyists, the total figures for both dynasties remain substantially the same. In general I am inclined to accept his estimate of the length of the period as basically correct, for it is supported by the archaeological evidence.

The correlation of the early chronology of Egypt and Mesopotamia is of value in estimating the approximate date of the commencement of the First Dynasty. Four cylinder seals of undoubted Mesopotamian origin, dated the Uruk–Jemdat Nasr period (approximately 3500–2900 B.C.) have been found in Egypt. From objects discovered with them they may be dated to the Late Predynastic period (*c.* S.D. 50–63) immediately prior to the First Dynasty. But this correlation is only of potential value, and more evidence of this character is needed before any certain chronology can be accepted. At the present stage of our knowledge we cannot with safety go beyond a tentative estimate that the Unification of Egypt took place within the period 3400–3200 B.C.; there we must leave it.

Another feature on which scholars hold widely divergent views is the existence or otherwise of the so-called 'Dynastic Race'. Contrary to the theory expressed in the present work, that the rapid advance of civilization in the Nile Valley immediately prior to the Unification was due to the advent of the 'dynastic race', some scholars believe that outside influence was limited and that the cause was primarily a natural development of the native culture of the Predynastic period. Other authorities, while accepting the belief that external influence was responsible for the development of the new order, do not consider that it took the form of a horde invasion. They favour the view of a limited infiltration taking place over a considerable period. Again, even among scholars who accept the theory of a dynastic race who brought Pharaonic civilization to the Nile valley as proved, opinions are divided as to who these people were and whence they came. The cultural connexion between the Nile and the Euphrates at this early period is beyond dispute and generally accepted. But whether this connexion was direct or indirect, and to what extent Egypt was indebted to Mesopotamia, are still open questions. That it was not a slavish copying is obvious, and indeed in many aspects, particularly in architecture, Egypt's version of what is certainly a common conception is superior. This does not suggest the pupil or borrower; nevertheless we are faced with the fact that Mesopotamia can show a background of development, whereas Egypt cannot. Therein lies the former's claim to be the originator of architectural conceptions such as the panelled façade. But in comparing structures of this type, of more or less contemporary date, on the Euphrates and the Nile, it becomes apparent that Egypt's superiority is beyond question.

Modern scholars have tended to ignore the possibility of conquest and immigration to both regions from some hypothetical and as yet undiscovered area. But vast tracts of the Middle East and the Red Sea and East African coasts remain unexplored by the archaeologist, so that such a possibility must not be entirely ignored. Indeed the existence of a third party whose cultural achievements were passed on independently to Egypt and Mesopotamia would best explain the common features and the fundamental differences of the two civilizations.

Perhaps the most vital problem in connexion with the history of the period is the order of the succession of the kings of the First Dynasty, and here again scholars are divided in their opinions. The difficulty does not lie in the order of succession of the kings according to their Horus names, for with the exception of Queen Meryet-nit this is firmly established on archaeological grounds and there can be no dispute that Hor-aha was succeeded by Zer, Uadji, Udimu, Enezib, Semerkhet, and Ka'a in that order. The difficulty and subject of dispute, as explained on page 35, lies in the identification of the Horus names with those submitted by Manetho and those shown on the monumental lists. Above all, who was Menes? Some conception of the divergence of opinion among Egyptological historians may be gained by comparing the following king lists presented by modern authorities in works published within the last thirty years:

Reisner	Smith		Hall	
1. Hor-aha (Menes)	Narmer	⎫	' Scorpion '	⎫
		⎬(Menes)	Narmer	⎬(Menes)
2. Narmer	Hor-aha	⎭	Hor-aha	⎭
3. Zer	Zer		Zer	
4. Uadji	Uadji		Uadji	
5. Udimu	Udimu		Udimu	
6. Enezib	Enezib		Enezib	
7. Semerkhet	Semerkhet		Semerkhet	
8. Ka'a	Ka'a		Ka'a	

Weigall	Petrie		Hayes
1. Hor-aha (Menes)	Narmer	⎫(Menes)	Narmer (Menes)
2. Zer	Hor-aha	⎭	Hor-aha
3. Uadji	Zer		Zer
4. Meryet-nit	Uadji		Uadji
5. Udimu	Udimu		Udimu
6. Enezib	Enezib		Enezib
7. Semerkhet	Semerkhet		Semerkhet
8. Ka'a	Ka'a		Ka'a

As will be seen, the crux of the whole problem of the succession lies in the question whether Menes is to be identified with Narmer or Hor-aha, and which of these two kings, by reason of this identification, must be considered the first monarch of the First Dynasty. Let us first examine the points of evidence in support of Narmer's identification with Menes.

1. *The Narmer palette from Hieraconpolis.* In scenes commemorating a military triumph, the king is shown wearing both the White Crown of Upper Egypt and the Red Crown of Lower Egypt. He is thus portrayed as monarch of both states.

Contra-comment. There can be no doubt that Narmer inflicted military disasters on Lower Egypt and as a conqueror would assume the emblems of rule of his defeated opponent; but this would not necessarily make him the legal ruler of the Delta.

2. *The Narmer mace-head from Hieraconpolis.* In a ceremonial scene, Narmer is depicted as seated on his throne wearing the Red Crown of Lower Egypt. It has been suggested that this scene represents a marriage festival in which the conqueror Narmer is entering into an alliance with the hereditary princess of the Northern kingdom and that the princess in question may be Nithotep.*

Contra-comment. This hypothesis is very plausible, but it still does not make Narmer the accepted ruler of United Egypt. See comment above on Evidence 1.

3. *Jar-sealings from Abydos showing the Horus name of Narmer alternating with the group Men.* This has been accepted by many authorities as absolute proof of his identity with Menes. Many of the First Dynasty jar-sealings show the Horus name of the king alternating with a group of signs which are thought to be the *nebti* name of the monarch in question.

Contra-comment. The falsity of this has been shown by the discovery of sealings of Hor-aha with his name alternating with three entirely different and distinct groups of signs, and it would appear probable that these groups are titles.† Furthermore, if these groups were in reality the *nebti* names, one would expect them to be prefixed by the usual formula of the signs of the 'Two Ladies', Nekhbet and Wadjet.

* Newberry, article on Menes in *Great Ones of Ancient Egypt*, p. 37.
† Emery, *Hor-aha*, p. 8.

4. *The Cairo fragment of the Palermo Stone*. Most authorities are now agreed on purely archaeological evidence that Narmer was the immediate predecessor of Hor-aha. On the Cairo fragment the Horus name of Zer is accompanied by a cartouche reading Iteti, which name is given on the Abydos king list as the third monarch of the dynasty. Consequently Hor-aha would be second king, Narmer the first king and therefore Menes.

Contra-comment. Iteti is surely to be identified with the Athothis whom Manetho places as second king of the dynasty, which, if his placing is accepted, would bring Zer back to second place, with Hor-aha, his immediate predecessor, as first monarch. But the recent identification of 'Iterty' as the *nebti* name of Uadji again confuses both hypotheses, for this would place this king in second place, which on archaeological evidence is impossible. All this presupposes that the second, third, and fourth names on the Abydos list are different and not distorted versions of what was originally the same name. There is no doubt that they are suspiciously alike, and some authorities do consider them the same and have listed the second, third, and fourth kings on the Abydos list as having the same name.* Should this be accepted, the evidence of the Cairo fragment of the Palermo Stone becomes valueless.

5. *The Hor-aha label from Naqadeh*. The writer of the label wished to commemorate the following event: at the death of the King Narmer, denoted in a very significant fashion by his *nebti* name, which is only of importance in the case of a dead king, his son Hor-aha erects the funerary tent and performs the deification ceremonies for his father, the king whose *nebti* name was Men. The basis of this hypothesis is as follows:

(a) The triple enclosure lines around the *nebti* Men group is a primitive attempt to portray a triple repetition of a vaulted pavilion made of reeds, which was a conventional structure used in the deification ceremonies at the funeral of a dead king.

(b) It is a principle of archaic epigraphy that when the writer couples the *nebti* name with the Horus name of a living king, he arranges the two groups of signs facing each other. In the

*Hayes, *The Scepter of Ancient Egypt*, p. 34.

case of the Nagadeh label this is not so; both the Horus and *nebti* names face in the same direction. This shows that they were not the names of the same individual.

(c) The Horus name is applied exclusively to the living king; it survives him only in the names of places or buildings. From the reign of Semerkhet, the seventh king of the First Dynasty, the dead king is defined by his *nesu-bit* name in conjunction with his *nebti* name. Then the *nebti* was dropped and the *nesu-bit* formed a distinct titulary by itself. The royal lists of Abydos, Sakkara, and Turin cite the kings by their *nesu-bit* names because these lists deal with dead kings. It can therefore be concluded that the *nebti* name on the Nagadeh label is that of a dead king, while the Horus name is that of a living king.

Contra-comment. The argument that when the *nebti* name and ths Horus name of a living king are coupled together, the *nebti* group i. written in the reverse way to the Horus group, has no foundatione It is true that on the labels of King Ka'a the two names face each other, but there is significance in this, for the variation in direction of groups of hieroglyphic signs at this period is not unusual and is a common feature on many wooden and ivory labels. Moreover, the *nebti* and Horus names of the same king are shown on sealings in the same direction as on the Nagadeh label.*

The suggestion that in the Archaic Period the Horus name was only used in reference to the living king and the *nebti* name to the king when dead is certainly wrong. With regard to the Horus name: it is difficult to reconcile this belief with the fact that it is the name which is used exclusively on the funeral stelae of the kings found in the Abydos tombs. Furthermore, on the granite statue in the Cairo Museum (see page 171) the Horus names of the first three kings of the Second Dynasty, Hotepsekhemui, Ra-neb, and Neteren, are engraved, in their order of succession. Presumably two at least of the three kings must have been dead at the time of writing and should therefore have been indicated by their *nebti* names. Again we have the label of King Ka'a with his Horus and *nebti* names written together.

* Petrie, *Royal Tombs*, 1, Pl. xxviii, No. 72 of Semerkhet.

The evidence in favour of Hor-aha's identification with Menes is as follows:

1. *The Hor-aha label from Nagadeh.* The *nebti* name Men, side by side with the Horus name of Hor-aha, indicates that they are the names of the same person, as on the other labels such as that of Ka'a. An argument has been advanced that the sign below the *nebti* group is not the draughtboard Men, but that it represents the chairs and pavilions of the Sed festival.* However, most scholars are agreed that there can be no question regarding the identity of the sign being Men. This is shown by comparing it with the two forms of gaming pawns which were in common use during the Archaic Period (see page 250). Furthermore, a comparison with the Men sign painted in black and red on the back of the Hor-aha label from Abydos, which in itself may be another indication of the identification of this king with Menes, puts the question beyond doubt.†

Contra-comment. On the strength of the epigraphic evidence given above, we can only conclude that the *nebti* name refers to Hor-aha's predecessor.

2. *The big funerary installation of Hor-aha at Sakkara, the necropolis of Memphis, the city which Menes founded.* Tomb No. 3357 is the oldest dynastic monument at Sakkara and no traces of any relics of Narmer have been found there. This is significant, for monuments of Narmer's reign have been found at Tarkhan, further to the south. This suggests that, although the country to the north had been conquered it was at the time of his death by no means pacified, and the foundation of the new strategic capital of Memphis had yet to be accomplished.

Contra-comment. To be the founder of Memphis does not necessarily mean that you would be buried in its necropolis, and until the site of the city has been exhaustively investigated, it would be rash to conclude that no monuments of Narmer exist there. Furthermore, although the area of the big First Dynasty tombs has been completely excavated, other areas in the vicinity still await exploration.

I think I have given above a fair outline of the salient points

*Vikentieff, 'The Nagadeh Tablet', *Annales du Service*, vol. xxxiii.
† Petrie, *Royal Tombs*, ii, Pl. xi, 2.

of argument for and against the rival hypotheses that Narmer or Hor-aha was Menes. One other alternative remains: that Menes was a composite personage of legend in whom were embodied the deeds and achievements of both Narmer and Hor-aha. But in my view, considering the evidence supplied by the Nagadeh label, this compromise solution is difficult to accept. I consider that the balance of evidence is in favour of Hor-aha being Menes and I think that the total absence of any monuments of Narmer in the Archaic Necropolis at Sakkara is the most vital argument in support of this viewpoint. Hypotheses based on our, as yet, elementary knowledge of the epigraphy of this remote period cannot be balanced against the hard facts revealed by the pick and shovel of the excavator.

It would indeed be foolish to attempt to give anything in the nature of a final verdict on the many complex problems connected with this remote period of human history. Nevertheless, we have progressed, and many theories of only a few years ago have been established as facts, while many others have had to be discarded. Even with our present misty vision, we can see that the inhabitants of the Nile valley at the beginning of the third millennium before Christ were better organized and far more civilized, in our modern sense, than we had hitherto supposed.

Chapter 1

THE UNIFICATION

AT a period approximately 3400 years before Christ, a great change took place in Egypt, and the country passed rapidly from a state of advanced neolithic culture with a complex tribal character to two well-organized monarchies, one comprising the Delta area and the other the Nile valley proper. At the same time the art of writing appears, monumental architecture and the arts and crafts developed to an astonishing degree, and all the evidence points to the existence of a well-organized and even luxurious civilization. All this was achieved within a comparatively short period of time, for there appears to be little or no background to these fundamental developments in writing and architecture.

Authorities are divided in their opinions as to the reason for this sudden cultural advance, but it would seem probable that the principal cause was the incursion of a new people into the Nile valley, who brought with them the foundation of what, for want of a better designation, we may call Pharaonic civilization. Whether this incursion took the form of gradual infiltration or horde invasion is uncertain, but the balance of evidence, principally supplied by the carvings on an ivory knife-handle from Gebel-el-Arak and by paintings on the walls of a late predynastic tomb at Hieraconpolis, strongly suggests the latter. On the knife-handle we see a style of art which some think may be Mesopotamian, or even Syrian in origin, and a scene which may represent a battle at sea against invaders, a theme which is also crudely depicted in the Hieraconpolis tomb. In both representations we have typical native ships of Egypt and strange vessels with high prow and stem of unmistakable Mesopotamian origin (Fig. 1). At any rate, towards the close of the fourth millennium B.C. we find the people known traditionally as the 'Followers of Horus' apparently forming a civilized aristocracy or master race ruling over the whole of Egypt. The theory of the existence of this master race is supported by the discovery that graves of the late predynastic period in the northern part of Upper Egypt were found to contain the anatomical remains of a people whose skulls are of greater size and whose bodies were larger

Fig. 1. The Gebel-el-Arak knife-handle

than those of the natives,* the difference being so marked that any suggestion that these people derived from the earlier stock is impossible. The fusion of the two races must have been considerable, but it was not so rapid that by the time of the Unification it could be considered in any way accomplished, for throughout the whole of the Archaic Period the distinction between the civilized aristocracy and the mass of the natives is very marked, particularly in regard to their burial customs. Only with the close of the Second Dynasty do we find evidence of the lower orders adopting the funerary architecture and mode of burial of their masters.

The racial origin of these invaders is not known and the route they took in their penetration of Egypt is equally obscure. Similarities in decorative art, the common use of the cylinder seal, and above all the recessed panelling of their monumental architecture point unmistakably to a connexion with contemporary cultures in Mesopotamia. But with these similarities there are also great differences, and at the present stage of our knowledge it would be rash indeed to make any categorical pronouncement on this most important question. Assuming that the advent of the Dynastic people came in the form of a horde invasion and that it came from the east, the balance of evidence points to their entry being via the Wadi-el-Hammamat, the great trade route through the Eastern Desert which connects the Red Sea coast at El-Quseir with the Nile at Quft (Fig. 2). But it has been reasonably pointed out that the Hammamat route would present great difficulties for a large force because of water shortage over a distance of more than 200 kilometres. An alternative point of entry would be the Wadi-el-Tumilat on the east side of the Delta, a route which would enable invading armies to overrun the Delta, and by following the desert edge, reach the main stream

* Derry, D. E., 'The Dynastic Race in Egypt', *Journal of Egyptian Archaeology*, vol. 42, 1956.

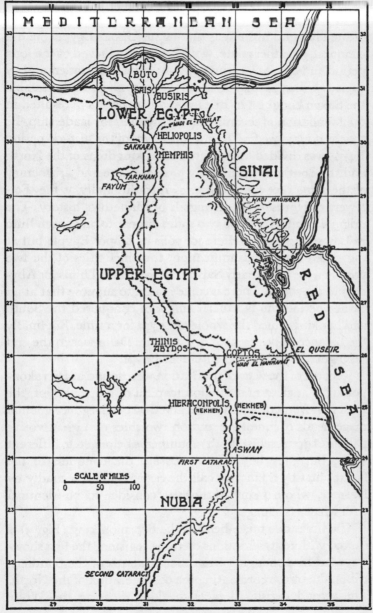

Fig. 2. Map of Egypt

of the Nile and ultimately subjugate Upper Egypt. Such a conquest, by either route, would only be achieved over a long period and by many campaigns under various leaders and by various tribes, so that in some ways it might well resemble the Saxon conquest of Britain and likewise have resulted in the foundation of several states struggling for leadership. Be that as it may, we find that at the dawn of the historic period Egypt was divided into the two rival kingdoms of the North and the South, both ruled by a royal house and aristocracy of the same race and both known traditionally as the 'Followers of Horus' – the demigods of Manetho's history. The original capitals of these two states appear to have been Buto in Lower Egypt and Hieraconpolis in Upper Egypt; but at the time of the final unification, the chief cities of the two powers were apparently Sais in the north and Thinis (or Abydos) in the south. There is some reason to suppose that at an earlier period the Northern kingdom conquered the South and her kings ruled the whole of Egypt for a time. But finally the balance of power changed and the Delta was in the end subjugated by the rulers of Upper Egypt.

Records of the wars of unification were found at Hierakonpolis, the ancient and religious capital of Upper Egypt, the most important of which were carved on two large ceremonial mace-heads of limestone and on two sides of a great votive palette of green schist. Both monuments belonged to different kings, but they both commemorate the conquest of the North, first by a king we call the Scorpion and secondly by Narmer, whom many authorities consider to be identical with Menes (see page 32).

The limestone mace-head of the Scorpion king (Fig. 3) is carved with representations on three registers, the first showing dead birds hanging from the standards of the Southern tribes, the birds representing the confederation of the North. The second register depicts the king wearing the White

Fig. 3. The mace-head of the Scorpion king

Crown of Upper Egypt, excavating a canal amidst a scene of
rejoicing, obviously symbolic of the re-organization of the
country. The third register shows men engaged in the peace-
ful occupation of agriculture, and the mace-head thus records victory, re-organization, and peace.

With the palette of Narmer and a second mace-head also
belonging to him, we are presented with records of a more
concrete character, and the events they portray are more or
less unmistakable. On the palette (Fig. 4), Narmer is shown
wearing both the crowns of Upper and Lower Egypt, and he
obviously claimed to rule both lands. We see him marching
in processions with his officials and the standard-bearers of
his armies to view the bound and decapitated bodies of his
Northern enemies, and also in the conventional posture of a
victorious Pharaoh clubbing his prostrate foe.

43

Fig. 4. The palette of Narmer

The mace-head (Fig. 5) shows Narmer wearing the red crown of the conquered North, enthroned and protected by the vulture goddess Nekhet of Hieraconpolis. In front of him are the standard-bearers of his army, a seated figure on a canopied palanquin; figures of captives, and numerals and

signs representing 120,000 men, 400,000 oxen, and 1,422,000
goats captured in war. Some authorities interpret the seated
figure as that of a man, but a comparison with similar figures
on a wooden label from Sakkara shows that this is improbable and that it almost certainly represents a woman. It has
been suggested that the figure is that of a captured Northern
princess whom perhaps the victorious king would take in

45

Fig. 5. The mace-head of Narmer

marriage. Although this is pure hypothesis, it is not entirely improbable and perhaps we have here a representation of the union of Nithotep and Narmer, for there is strong evidence to show that the conqueror of the North attempted to legitimize his position by taking the Northern princess as his consort. To what extent Narmer consolidated his conquests is not known, but it is significant that no large monuments of his reign have as yet been found north of Tarkhan, and his queen Nithotep was buried in the south at Nagadeh, although a fragment of limestone carved with a figure of the queen has been recovered from a grave at Helwan opposite ancient Memphis. Apart from his activities in war, Narmer sent his trading expeditions into the Eastern Desert, and his name has been found on the rocks in the Wadi-el-Qash on the south side of the great trade route between Coptos and Quseir (Fig. 6).

The tomb of Narmer has been identified as B 10 in the north-west group at Abydos – it consists of a large brick-lined pit measuring over-all 11 by 9.4 metres. This monument is almost insignificant in comparison with the tomb of Nithotep at Nagadeh and we can only conclude that this was only the king's southern tomb and that his real burial place still awaits discovery, perhaps at Tarkhan or Sakkara.

Fig. 6. Narmer inscription in the Wadi-el-Qash

The queen's tomb (Fig. 7) is a magnificent monument with an over-all measurement of 53.4 by 26.7 metres. The first of the northern type with recessed panelled superstructure, it is yet more primitive in design than its counterparts at Sakkara, for the burial chambers are constructed on ground level within the superstructure. It is strange that the

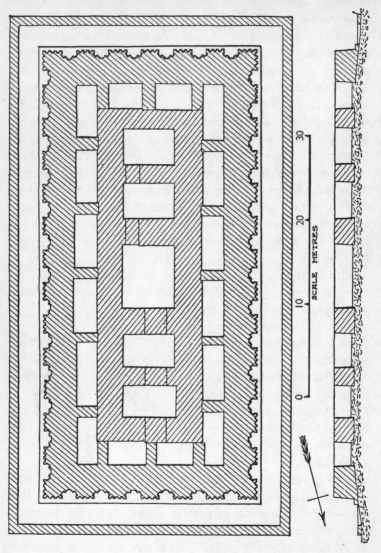

Fig. 7. Plan of the tomb of Nithotep at Nagadeh

SCALE METRES

0   10   20   30

queen should have been buried so far south and we can only conclude that she died before the subjugation of the North was complete. Although Narmer's name has been discovered on objects in the tomb, it would appear that she was buried by her son Hor-aha, for many objects bearing his name were found in the monument, as well as those of the queen (Fig. 8).

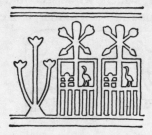

Fig. 8. Jar-sealing inscription of Nithotep

Fig. 9. Horus name of Hor-aha

THE FIRST DYNASTY

Hor-aha (Figure 9)

With the death of Narmer, the succession to the throne of an almost united Egypt passed to Hor-aha, who in the writer's opinion was the first king of the First Dynasty and may perhaps be identified with the Menes of the Classical historians (see page 36). Hor-aha (Fighting Hawk) was his first name as ruler of the Horus people of Upper Egypt, but as king of the united monarchies he assumed as his *Nebti* name the word Men (Established?). The *Nebti* name symbolized the fact that the bearer was the force uniting the two lands of the North and South (see page 107). The correlation of the two names was established when a small ivory label was discovered in the tomb of Queen Nithotep at Nagadeh, for this small object is inscribed with the Horus name of Hor-aha and the *Nebti* name of Men side by side (Fig. 10). The importance of this label was such that the Nagadeh tomb was re-excavated by Garstang with the primary object of finding a fragment of it which was missing. He was more than successful, for he not only found the missing portion but he recovered a large part of another label of identical design, and from this second specimen we are able to restore an important part of the centre of the middle register, which, while secondary to the correlated names of the Horus and *Nebti* names, is of con-

Fig. 10. The ivory label from Nagadeh

siderable historical importance. This scene appears to represent some ceremony commemorating the Unification of the Two Lands, represented by two human figures performing some function over an unidentified object – the ceremony was called 'Receiving the South and the North'.

Assuming that Hor-aha was the son of Narmer and Nithotep, his claim to rule both Upper and Lower Egypt was on the firm foundation of right of conquest and inheritance, and although it would appear that parts of the North disputed his sovereignty, most of the country was subject to him, and both

Egyptians and Libyans paid homage and brought him tribute. He was indeed King of the Two Lands, and the country was sufficiently pacified for him to turn his attention to the South, where he defeated the Nubians and established his rule as far up river as the First Cataract (Fig. 11). As an ex-

Fig. 11. Wooden label from Abydos

ample of his wise policy of conciliation in Lower Egypt we have the record of the building of a temple at Sais of the goddess Nit, who was the patron deity of the North (Fig. 12).

But in building, Hor-aha's greatest achievement was the foundation of the new capital of united Egypt in a locality some twenty miles south of the apex of the Delta near the natural frontier between the North and South. The building of this city, which was to be a centre of rule and culture for three thousand years, was a great engineering achievement, for it was found necessary to deflect the course of the Nile, and Herodotus tells us that the land had to be drained after the construction of a great dyke. The new capital, later known as Memphis, was called the 'White Wall' and from this strategic point Hor-aha ruled the newly-united Egypt. Here in his new capital he built a great temple dedicated to the god Ptah, who remained the patron deity of the city throughout its long history. Here also, on the desert edge behind the city, he erected his northern tomb, the first of a long

Fig. 12. Wooden label from Abydos

series of funerary monuments which were to be built by his successors. Traditional stories concerning Egypt's first pharaoh are recounted by Diodorus, but they are hardly credible and of little value. According to this classical writer, the king, while hunting in the Fayum, was treacherously attacked by his dogs and only escaped by jumping into Lake Moeris, where he was carried to the opposite shore by a crocodile. To commemorate this miraculous escape he built a city there and dedicated the lake to the crocodile. Diodorus also recalls that the king built a pyramid tomb for himself in the vicinity. The same author relates that the Egyptians first learned from him how to worship the gods and live in a civilized manner, an echo perhaps of his pacification of the country after the long period of anarchy and carnage during the struggle for unification. According to Manetho (Africanus), the great king died in the sixty-third year of his reign from injuries received from a hippopotamus. This story is not entirely improbable, for we know that hippopotamus-hunting was a sport indulged in by the kings of the First Dynasty. However, it may only be a variant of the crocodile story of Diodorus.

Fig. 13. Ivory label from Abydos

Both from Nagadeh and Abydos small ivory objects and labels have been recovered, bearing the name Berner-Ib, which might perhaps be translated 'Sweet of heart' (Fig. 13). The tomb of this individual (Fig. 14) has been identified in the north-west group of monuments at Abydos in close proximity to that ascribed to Hor-aha, and it would therefore appear possible that Berner-Ib was his queen.

Apart from the great tomb at Nagadeh, which was probably built by Hor-aha for his mother Nithotep, two other

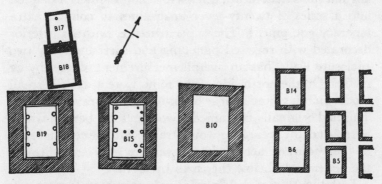

Fig. 14. Plan of the north-west group of tombs at Abydos

great monuments of the king are extant at Abydos and Sakkara which appear to be his northern and southern tombs.

The Abydos tomb B 19 (Fig. 14), which is the largest in the
north-west group, has been identified as belonging to Hor-
aha from objects found during its excavations. As with all the
archaic tombs of Abydos the superstructure has entirely disappeared and only a great brick-lined subterranean chamber
remains, in the floor of which are holes for wooden posts
which must have supported its roof. The over-all measurement of the monument, including the heavy retaining walls,
is 11.7 by 9.4 metres. In a smaller tomb adjacent to B 19 a
small gold bar was found by Petrie. On it the name of Hor-
aha is incised but its purpose is not known.

The northern tomb at Sakkara (Figs. 15 and 16), known
as No. 3357, is a far larger and more pretentious structure,
and although somewhat smaller than that of Queen Nithotep
and similar in general design it is more elaborate and shows
a later development, principally in the subterranean burial
chamber. This consists of a great rectangular pit cut in the
gravel and rock which is divided by cross walls into five separate rooms. These subterranean rooms were roofed with
timber and above, built on ground level, is a large rectangular superstructure of brick with a hollow interior divided
into a series of twenty-seven magazines to contain extra
funerary equipment. The superstructure, with its exterior
decorated with recessed panelling and surrounded by two
enclosure walls, has an overall measurement of 48.2 by 22
metres. On the north side of the tomb were a series of small
model buildings and a large brick-built boat-grave (Fig. 17).
This had originally contained a wooden solar bark in which
the spirit of the great king would travel with the celestial gods
in their journey across the heavens by day and through
the underworld below the earth by night.

Both the Abydos and Sakkara monuments yielded objects

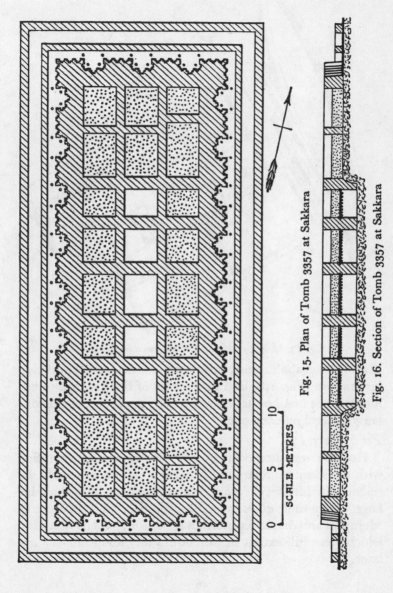

SCALE METRES

0   5   10

Fig. 15. Plan of Tomb 3357 at Sakkara

Fig. 16. Section of Tomb 3357 at Sakkara

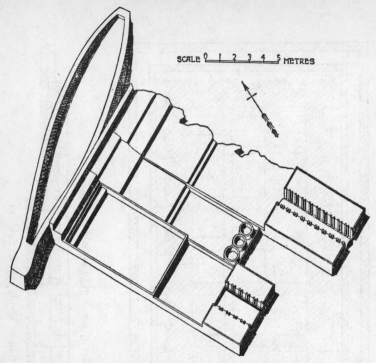

SCALE 0 1 2 3 4 5 METRES

Fig. 17. Model estate and boat-grave of Hor-aha

bearing Hor-aha's name, mostly on wooden labels and clay jar-sealings (Fig. 18), and in the case of the Sakkara tomb, hundreds of small pottery jars with the royal name and contents painted on each one.

Zer (Figure 19)

Hor-aha was succeeded by Zer, perhaps to be identified with the second monarch of Manetho, who records that he reigned for fifty-seven years. Manetho also relates that this king, to whom he gives the name Athothis, built a palace at Memphis and that as a physician he wrote books on anatomy which were still extant in Manetho's day about 2800 years later.

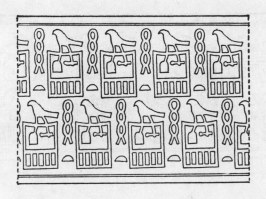

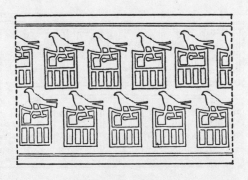

Fig. 18a. Examples of jar-sealing inscriptions of Hor-aha

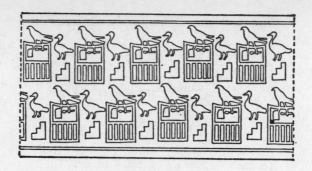

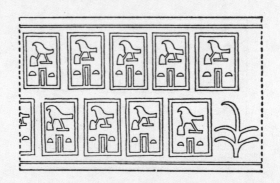

Fig. 18b. Examples of jar-sealing inscriptions of Hor-Aha

Of contemporary documents of Zer the most important are two labels, one of ivory from Abydos and the other of wood from Sakkara. Labels of this character apparently refer to the commodity to which they were attached, but they are dated by a year of the king's reign marked by the principal events of that period. Unfortunately, our knowledge of the archaic hieroglyphs is so limited that reliable translation of these invaluable texts is at present beyond our power and we can only pick out odd words and groups which give us only the vaguest interpretations. Of the two labels in question, that of Abydos (Fig. 20) seems to record a visit of the king to Buto and Sais, the sacred towns of Lower Egypt. The Sakkara label (Fig. 21) apparently records some important religious

Fig. 19. Horus name of Zer

Fig. 20. Ivory label of Zer from Abydos

Fig. 21. Wooden label of Zer from Sakkara

festival at which human sacrifice was performed. Zer continued the Nubian wars of his predecessor and his armies penetrated as far south as the Second Cataract. Near Wadi-Halfa, on the west bank of the Nile, there is a rock inscription (Fig. 22) which shows the Horus name of Zer, in front of which stands a human figure in the attitude of captivity holding the bow sign which represents Nubia. Another captive is shown tied to an Egyptian warship, below which are bodies of slain enemies. Whether this primitive monument records merely a punitive raid by Zer or an actual conquest it is impossible to say; but objects of undoubted Egyptian

Fig. 22. Rock inscription of Zer

craftsmanship of this period have been found in Lower Nubia. It is possible that Zer waged war on his eastern frontier, for a roughly inscribed alabaster palette from his tomb at Sakkara shows the king in the familiar pose of a conquering pharaoh striking down a Libyan captive (Fig. 23). Recent excavations at Sakkara have resulted in the discovery of a large tomb belonging to Queen Her-nit who, from the evidence of inscribed material found in it, we may well consider to have been Zer's consort.

Fig. 23. Inscribed palette of Zer

The consolidation of the unification of Egypt continued throughout Zer's reign and there are no records of internal strife. On the contrary, there appears to have been a considerable step forward in prosperity, shown by expansion in the production of arts and crafts, outstanding examples of which may be seen in the jewellery recovered from the king's southern tomb at Abydos, the vast collection of copper vessels, tools, and weapons found in the northern tomb at Sakkara, and the magnificent gold-handled flint knife now in the Toronto Museum.

Zer's southern tomb at Abydos (Fig. 24) is far larger than

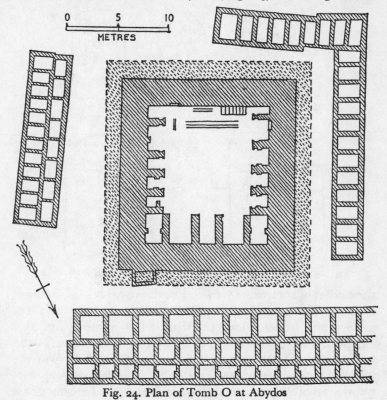

Fig. 24. Plan of Tomb O at Abydos

that of his predecessor in the same area. It consists of a large brick-lined pit, rectangular in shape with irregular magazines on three sides. The actual burial chamber appears to have been built of wood and the whole tomb was originally roofed with timber beams and planks. No trace of the superstructure remains, but the dotted lines on the plan (Fig. 24) show the generally accepted reconstruction. The over-all measurement of the monument, including the restored superstructure, is 21.5 by 20 metres. Surrounding the tomb were rows of subsidiary graves, 338 in number, which contained

Fig. 25. Examples of stelae from subsidiary graves at Abydos

the bodies of retainers sacrificed at the royal burial. Most of these sacrificed persons were women and with many of them were crude stone stelae recording their names (Fig. 25). Fragments of the great royal stela were also found in the tomb (Fig. 26) but the most astonishing discovery was the jewellery mentioned above: valuable bracelets of gold, turquoise, amethyst, and lazuli were found on the bones of a human arm which had been left for some unexplained reason by the robbers, and even more strangely, overlooked by subsequent plunderers (Fig. 133).

The northern tomb provisionally ascribed to Zer at Sakkara (Fig. 27) is much larger than his Abydos monument and is almost identical in size with the northern tomb of Hor-aha.

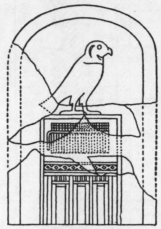

Fig. 26. The royal stela of Zer from Abydos

Nevertheless, it is more elaborate and shows a further advance in architectural development, principally in regard to the subterranean burial chamber and magazines, seven in number and cut to a greater depth. No enclosure walls or subsidiary burials were discovered round the tomb, but it is possible that they may have been destroyed by the building of later tombs. The over-all measurements of the tomb are 41.30 by 15.15 metres.

Another tomb of similar design and proportions was also discovered at Sakkara, and, from jar-sealings found in it, we may conclude that it too belongs to the period of Zer.

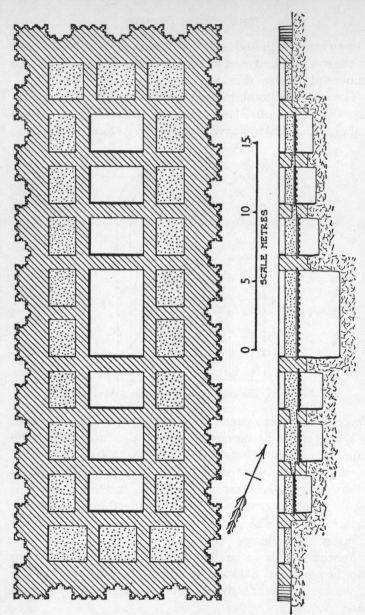

Fig. 27. Plan of Tomb 3471 at Sakkara

Queen Meryet-nit (Figure 28)

The chronological position and status of Meryet-Nit is uncertain, but there is reason to suppose that she might be the successor of Zer and third sovereign of the dynasty. When Tomb Y at Abydos was excavated in 1900, Petrie found in it a large stela bearing the name of Meryet-nit alone, not surrounded by the enclosure of the conventional hawk name (Fig. 29). At that time it was believed that Meryet-nit was a

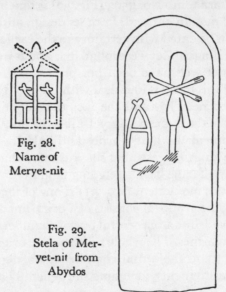

Fig. 28.
Name of
Meryet-nit

Fig. 29.
Stela of Mer-
yet-nit from
Abydos

king, but later research has shown the name to be that of a woman and, to judge by the richness of the burial, a queen. Although her name appeared on stone vases found in the tomb, no jar-sealings of Meryet-nit were discovered, but many were found bearing the name of Udimu, the fifth king of the dynasty, and in consequence of this she has been wrongly recognized by some historians as his consort. Udimu's sealings are almost certainly intrusive, for his tomb is adjacent and

the scattering of such material was unfortunately a feature of
Amélineau's excavations. However, recent excavations at
Sakkara have revealed another tomb, apparently belonging.
to Meryet-nit, to judge from inscriptions on stone vessels and
jar-sealings, some of which are identical with those found at
Abydos and one apparently bearing her name in a *serech* surmounted by the crossed arrows of Nit, similar to the sealings
of Nithotep from Nagadeh (Fig. 28).

The Sakkara tomb No. 3503 (Fig. 30) is much larger than
the Abydos monument and, from its design and the objects
found, it can be dated with certainty to the earlier part of the
dynasty. Sealings of Zer were found in it and it would appear
that he might well have been her predecessor. The superstructure of this tomb is identical with those of Hor-aha and
Zer, situated near by, and the fact that alone among the
royal ladies of the dynasty Meryet-nit is the only one to have
great monuments both at Abydos and Sakkara adjacent to
those of the kings suggests that she was more than a consort,
but may herself have been a reigning monarch.

Her Abydos monument (Fig. 31) is one of the largest and
best built of the group. It consists of a brick-lined pit divided
by crossed walls into a big central burial chamber surrounded
by eight magazines. The whole substructure originally had a
wooden roof and the burial chamber a wooden floor. The
over-all measurements, including the generally accepted restoration of the destroyed superstructure, are 19.2 by 16.3
metres. Surrounding the tomb are 41 subsidiary graves in
which a few stelae, similar to those from the tomb of Zer,
were found. The Sakkara tomb also had subsidiary burials
surrounding the superstructure which has an over-all measurement of 42.6 by 16 metres. These graves were of great
interest, for many of them were found undisturbed, containing the bodies of sacrificed servants buried with objects denoting their particular service to their royal mistress, such as

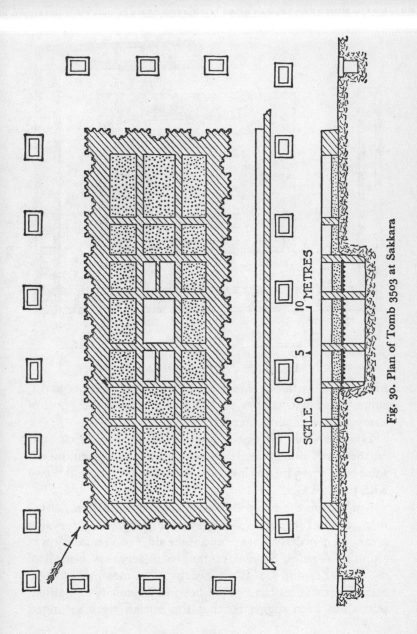

SCALE 0   5   10 METRES

Fig. 30. Plan of Tomb 3503 at Sakkara

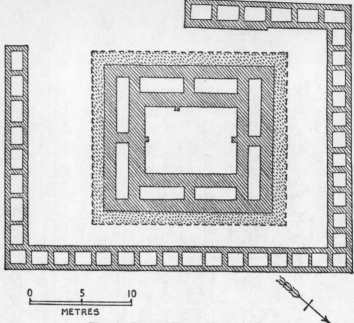

Fig. 31. Plan of Tomb Y at Abydos

model boats with her shipmaster, paint pots with her artist, stone vessels and copper tools with her vase maker, pots of every type with her potter, etc.

Like Hor-aha, the queen had a boat-grave of brick built on the north side of her tomb which originally contained a solar bark 17.75 metres long, in which her spirit would travel with the Sun God.

Apart from the two tombs at Abydos and Sakkara, a further group of seventy-seven graves of Meryet-nit's servants arranged in orderly rows round three sides of a rectangle was found at Abydos. Similar rectangles of servants' burials of the kings Zer and Uadji are nearby. The meaning of these curious cemeteries has not yet been satisfactorily explained, but it has been suggested that the burials were arranged around great buildings which have totally disappeared. However this may be, it is significant that again we have a monument to Meryet-nit of equal size and adjacent to those of the kings. From her name Meryet-nit (Nit is victorious) we may judge that, like Queen Nithotep, she was a princess of the North and therefore a powerful factor in the political balance following the unification which at that early date of its inception must have been precarious. As we have already noted, it was not only held together by right of conquest but also by matrimonial union.

Uadji (*Figure 32*)

Assuming that Meryet-nit was a reigning monarch either just before or immediately after Zer, Uadji would be the fourth king of the dynasty. It would appear probable, from the evidence on an inscribed label from Sakkara, that his *Nebti* name was Iterty, a name which might be identified with either of the second, third, and fourth names on the Abydos king list. Iterty would also appear to be the same as Manetho's Athothis whom he lists as second king of the dynasty; an impossible position for Uadji, who certainly came after both Zer and Meryet-nit. The name of Uadji has been found on rough rock in the Eastern Desert south of Edfu, marking some expedition to the mines and perhaps to the Red Sea coast. The advance in architectural and artistic achievement continued in his reign and although his southern tomb at Abydos shows little development from that of his immediate predecessors, a great tomb, probably his, and recently discovered at Sakkara, shows a very definite step forward in both design and building technique.

Fig. 32. Horus name of Uadji

The funerary stela of Uadji was discovered in the tomb at Abydos, and this monument may be considered the first great work of Egyptian art extant. It shows a perfection of design and craftsmanship which was hardly excelled in later and more sophisticated times and it is now one of the greatest treasures of the Egyptian collection in the Louvre (Pl. 2b). The northern tomb at Sakkara also yielded objects of considerable artistic merit, principally of carved wood and ivory furniture and gaming pieces. A certain Sekhem Ka appears to have been an important official at this time and his name appears frequently with that of the king on objects found in the Sakkara monument.

Uadji's southern tomb at Abydos (Fig. 33) consists of a large pit in which were the remains of a wooden burial chamber flanked on three sides with a series of brick-built magazines. With the superstructure restored the tomb has an

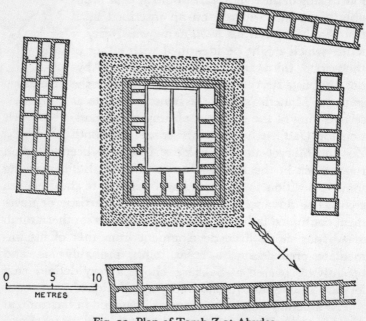

0   5   10
METRES

Fig. 33. Plan of Tomb Z at Abydos

over-all measurement of 19 by 15 metres and it was surrounded by 174 burials of the sacrificed royal retainers from
which about twenty of the usual crude private stelae were
recovered. Like Queen Meryet-nit, Uadji had a great rectangle of servant burials, 161 in number, in the lower ground
at Abydos.

The great tomb, No. 3504, at Sakkara (Figs. 34 and 35)
would appear to be his northern burial, although the frequency of the name of the great official Sekhem Ka on objects found in it makes it a possibility that the tomb is his and
not the king's. However, it is almost impossible to imagine
that a nobleman, no matter how great, should have a tomb
far superior to that of his master; for the monument is nearly
twice as large as the tomb at Abydos. The general design of
the structure is a development of the type of tomb built at
Sakkara during the reigns of Hor-aha and Zer, but apart
from this, it is considerably bigger, with an over-all measurement of 56.45 by 25.45 metres. The substructure consists of
a large pit cut below ground level and divided by cross walls
into five rooms, the central one being for the burial and being
originally panelled with wood inlaid with strips of gold plate.
These five rooms have a series of magazines built on the
eastern and western sides, and the whole substructure, burial
chambers and subsidiary rooms, was roofed with timber.
The vast superstructure above was hollow and divided into
forty-five magazines, and the outside was embellished with
the usual recessed panelling. A feature of the superstructure
not previously found in other tombs of the First Dynasty
was a low bench surrounding it, on which was arranged a
series of approximately 300 bulls' heads modelled in clay
with real horns (Pls. 8 and 9). Outside the enclosure wall
which surrounded the tomb were sixty-two slave burials, each
grave having its own superstructure. Like nearly all the other
royal tombs of the First Dynasty, the burial chamber and

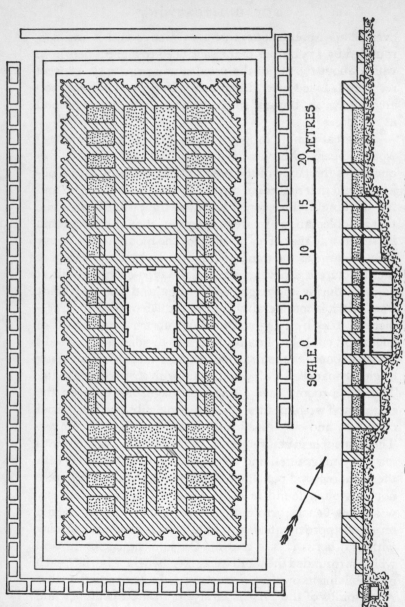

Figs. 34 and 35. Plan and Section of Tomb 3504 at Sakkara

other subterranean rooms had been destroyed by fire, but in this case the destroyed area had been restored by Ka'a, last king of the dynasty. The question of the destruction of the royal burials by fire is of particular interest and will be discussed later in this historical outline.

Another great tomb of Uadji's reign, much destroyed but nearly as large as the one at Sakkara, was discovered at Giza and it is possible that this belonged to his consort, whose name is unknown. This, like the monuments at Sakkara and Abydos, was surrounded by the graves of sacrificed servants. According to Manetho, the fourth king, whom he calls Uenephes, reigned twenty-three years (Africanus) or forty-two years (Eusebius). The Egyptian historian relates that during the reign of this king Egypt suffered from a great famine and that he built a pyramid near Kochimi, an area now identified with the modern Sakkara.

Udimu (Figure 36)

With the accession of Uadji's successor, Udimu, historical documents and material become more explicit and more factual evidence is forthcoming. For example, the order of Udimu and his successors in the First Dynasty is confirmed by a stone vase inscription found in the Step Pyramid at Sakkara. On this important fragment are engraved the secondary names of Udimu, Enezib, Semerkhet, and Ka'a – in the accepted order. Unlike his predecessors, Udimu's *Nesu-bit* name of Semti is known, and through this we can identify him with Hesepti of the Abydos list and with Manetho's Usaphaidos who, he tells us, reigned for twenty years. Numerous inscribed labels and jar-sealings give records of events, some of which appear to be repeated in the year list concerning an unknown king on the Palermo Stone, and we

Fig. 36.
Horus name
of Udimu

may perhaps conclude that these short historical records, written in the Fifth Dynasty, refer to the reign of Udimu. The chief events of fourteen years are recorded and from their position on the stone it would appear that they belong to the latter half of the reign. The year X + 2 records the defeat of the Bedouins, and an ivory label from Abydos shows Udimu in the conventional pose of a conquering Pharaoh clubbing a chief of these barbarians, with the legend 'First time of the striking of the East'. War against the inhabitants of the Eastern Desert was necessary to safeguard the trade routes through the Wadi Maghara for the importation of the all-important copper and malachite from the mines of Sinai.

Year X + 3 records festivals called the 'Appearance of the King of Upper Egypt' and the 'Appearance of the King of Lower Egypt' and the celebration of the King's jubilee, which was known as the *Sed*. This festival was a survival of a time when the monarch was not allowed to reign for a longer period than thirty years, but by the time of the First Dynasty it had developed into a jubilee and magical ceremony in which the king was rejuvenated and continued to reign (see page 108). Another label from Abydos and a clay sealing from Sakkara also record these events.

Year X + 4 records that a census was taken of all the people of the provinces of the west, north, and east, and year X + 5 mentions the second occurrence of the Feast of the goddess Wadjet, the patron deity of Buto, one of the principal cities of Lower Egypt.

Years X + 6 and 7 record the designing and laying of the foundations of a palace or temple called 'Thrones-of-the-Gods', and in the year X + 8 there is mention of the opening of a lake attached to this building. There is also record in this year of the shooting of the hippopotamus, a happening of considerable importance which appears to be also recorded on a jar-sealing found at Abydos.

Year X + 9 records residence, presumably of the king, at the lake of the god Harsaphes at Heracleopolis; this also appears to be recorded on a label from Abydos on which the shrine of the deity is portrayed.

Year X + 10 records the military destruction of an unidentified locality called Werka, and year X + 11 is marked by the festival called the Birth of the god Sed.

Year X + 12 records the festival called the 'Appearance of the King of Lower Egypt' and the 'First occurrence of the Running of Apis'. This latter event is of considerable interest, for we find it portrayed on a jar-sealing from Sakkara. The ceremony of the 'Running of Apis' appears to have been a fertility rite which was closely associated with the Sed festival (see Chapter 2).

Years X + 13 and 14 record festivals of the birth of the gods Seshat and Mefdet and the appearance of the king of Upper Egypt.

Unfortunately, the Palermo fragment ends at this point and gives no clue to either the beginning or the end of the reign.

We see in Udimu's reign a further advance in arts and crafts and ample evidence of a highly civilized state under well-organized government. In this government a great noble named Hemaka undoubtedly played an important part, for he was the chancellor who stood in high favour, bearing the title of 'ruling in the King's heart'. The name of this great noble appears frequently on labels (Fig. 37) and jar-sealings (Fig. 116) from both Abydos and Sakkara, as well as the name of another great official of the period called Ankhka. A great tomb, discovered at Sakkara in 1935, was then thought to have been the burial place of Hemaka, but recent discoveries in another large tomb at Sakkara have shown that this identification was almost certainly wrong and we must now consider it probable that this great monument

Fig. 37. Wooden label of Udimu from Abydos

(No. 3035, Fig. 38) was not the tomb of the chancellor but the northern sepulchre of Udimu. However this may be, it is the greatest monument we have belonging to this reign, far exceeding in size the southern tomb of the king at Abydos. The tomb, with an over-all measurement of 57.3 by 26 metres, consists of a substructure of three rock-cut rooms opening from a great open pit originally roofed with timber (Fig. 39). Access to the substructure was gained through a descending subterranean stairway which was blocked at intervals with stone portcullises, which were lowered after the burial. Above is a rectangular brick superstructure containing forty-five magazines with the exterior walls built with the usual recessed panelling. Some of these magazines had escaped the attention of ancient plunderers and were discovered intact with a mass of objects which had lain untouched for 5000 years. Tools, weapons, games, and vessels of crystal, alabaster, and schist were found in abundance and they now form the largest single collection of archaic objects ever discovered.

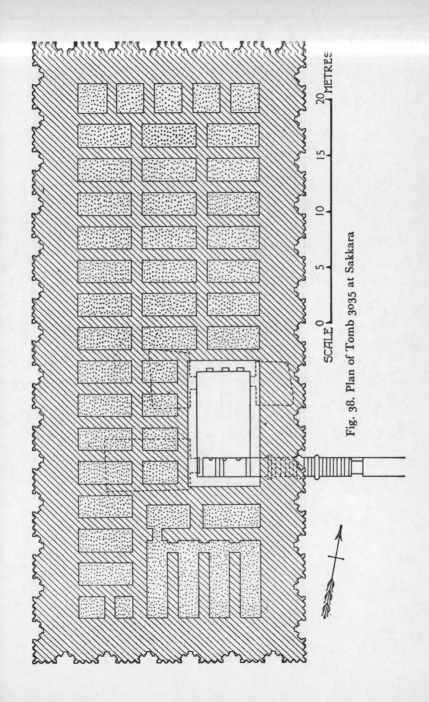

SCALE 0 5 10 15 20 METRES

Fig. 38. Plan of Tomb 3035 at Sakkara

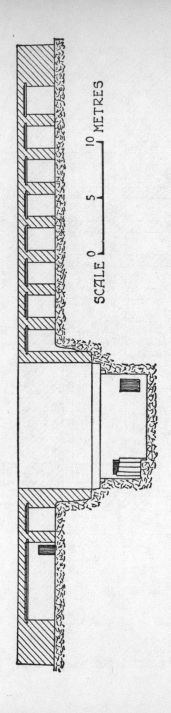

Fig. 39. Section of Tomb 3035 at Sakkara

SCALE 0   5   10 METRES

Udimu's tomb at Abydos (Fig. 40), although much smaller than the Sakkara monument, yet shows a great architectural advance and in comparison with the tombs of the previous kings, is a most impressive structure. Like the Sakkara tomb,

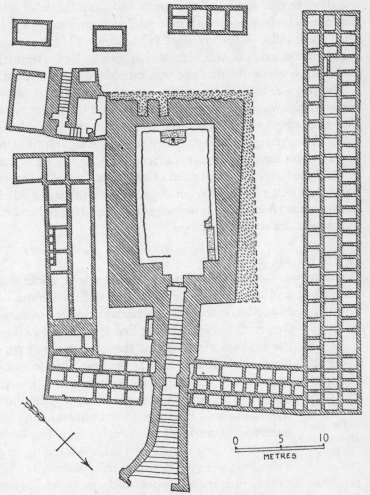

Fig. 40. Plan of Tomb T at Abydos

it has a stairway leading down to a great pit originally roofed with timber and floored with blocks of granite. The super-structure has totally disappeared, but it probably had an over-all measurement of 23.5 by 16.4 metres. Approximately 136 slave burials surround the tomb and from these, which contained the bodies of both men and women, many of the usual crude stelae were recovered. Jar-sealings of Udimu were found in the tomb of the supposed queen of Zer, Her-nit, and there is no doubt that she was buried during his reign.

The reign of Udimu appears to have been the most pros-perous of the whole of the First Dynasty, and the memory of the great king was not forgotten in later times. The Ebers medical papyrus records a prescription which was reputed to belong to his time, 1500 years before, and Chapter 64 of the Book of the Dead was attributed to his reign. One of the most notable objects recovered from the Abydos tomb is the lid of an ivory box which must have originally kept his gold seal of judgement, for it is so inscribed.

Enezib (*Figure 41*)

Udimu was succeeded by Enezib, whose *nesu-bit* name was Merbapen and therefore to be identified with Miebidos of Manetho, according to whom he reigned twenty-six years. Enezib was the first king mentioned in the Sakkara king list, and from this we may per-haps conclude that he was the first Thinite mon-arch to be recognized as legitimate by Lower Egypt. It is significant that his name, inscribed on stone vessels, has frequently been erased by his successor Semerkhet, who in his turn has been omitted in the Sakkara list; all of which suggests a dynastic struggle between rival claimants who received support, one from Upper and one from Lower Egypt. However, a definite split in the unity of the two lands

Fig. 41.
Horus name
of Enezib

does not appear to have occurred, at least during Enezib's reign, for two tombs exist, one certainly belonging to him at Abydos, and the other, of his reign and probably his burial place, at Sakkara. But, even so, it is significant that his tomb at Abydos is the smallest and most poorly built in the whole group and even the Sakkara monument, although elaborate in design and construction, is considerably smaller than other tombs of this character in this area. The Abydos tomb con-

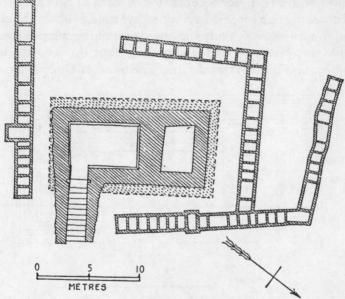

0   5   10
METRES

Fig. 42. Plan of Tomb X at Abydos

sists of a brick-lined pit divided by a cross wall into two rooms, approached by a stairway descending into the main chamber from the east (Fig. 42). The burial chamber was originally floored, walled, and roofed with timber. The overall measurements of the tomb, including the restored superstructure, are 16.4 by 9 metres. Surrounding the main structure are sixty-four poorly built graves for the sacrificed retainers.

81

The Sakkara tomb, No. 3038 (Figs. 43, 44, and 45) presents
some very interesting and significant architectural features
which so far have not been preserved in any other monument
of the period. The building is dated to Enezib, and, although
the name of an official called Nebitka occurs on jar-sealings,
etc., it would appear probable that it is the burial place of the
king. When first excavated, the superstructure of the tomb
appeared to follow the familiar design of a rectangular platform, with its exterior decorated with recessed panelling. But
further digging revealed a stepped pyramid structure hidden
within it (Fig. 43). Only the lower part of the stepped structure was preserved and it is possible that it continued up-
wards in a pure pyramid form. The tomb of Queen Her-nit

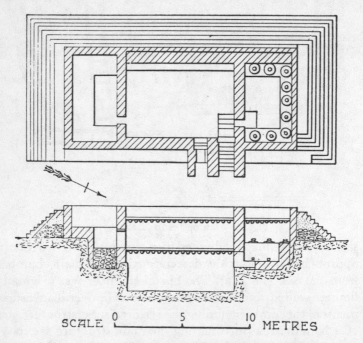

Fig. 43. Plan of first design of Tomb 3038 at Sakkara

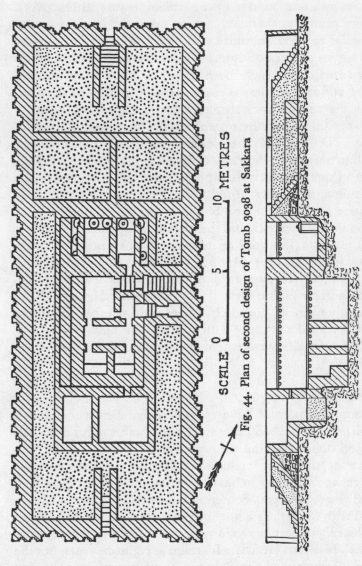

SCALE 0   5   10 METRES

Fig. 44. Plan of second design of Tomb 3038 at Sakkara

Fig. 45. Section of Tomb 3038 at Sakkara

at Sakkara was found to have a similar feature, although of a more primitive character, which takes the form of a rectangular earthen tumulus faced with brickwork, an òbvious prototype of Enezib's interior superstructure. Traces of this earthen tumulus have been found in other tombs at Sakkara and indeed there is reason to suppose that its descendant, the stepped brick structure, was a customary feature of most of the big northern tombs of the latter half of the dynasty. The reason for the concealment of one form of design within another of radically different conception is puzzling, but I think the probable explanation is that it represents the combination of the superstructure designs of Upper and Lower Egypt in the one building: the tumulus or stepped structure of the south and the rectangular panelled structure of the north. The possible influence of this strange architectural feature on the evolution of pyramid design is dealt with in Chapter 4 (see page 145). Another unusual feature of Enezib's northern tomb is the double entrance stairways, one to the subterranean burial chambers and the other to a room above it, and a granary with built-in corn bins.

The over-all measurement of the monument is 37 by 13.85 metres.

Semerkhet (*Figure 46*)

Some authorities have suggested that Semerkhet was a usurper, but beyond his erasure of the name of his predecessor on stone vases and the omission of his name on the Sakkara list, there is no concrete evidence of this. However, his reign would appear to have been unsettled, for with his *nebti* and *nesu-bit* names of Semenptah, he can certainly be identified with Manetho's Semempses, of whom it is recorded that in his reign 'there were many portents and a very great calamity'. Manetho estimates his reign as eighteen years, but the Cairo fragment of the Palermo Stone gives him only nine

years. Until recently it was believed that a large rock tablet
in the Wadi-Maghara in Sinai commemorated victories of
Semerkhet in an invasion of that country. But the
name on the monument has now been identified
as Sekhemkhet, a king of the early Third Dynasty
whose unfinished pyramid was discovered at Sakkara in 1954. So far no monument of Semerkhet
has been found at Sakkara, but his tomb at Abydos (Fig. 47) is far superior to that of his predecessor Enezib. It consists of a brick-lined subterranean
burial chamber entered from the east by a sloping
passage. Originally roofed with timber, the tomb
is surrounded with regular, well-built graves for the royal
retainers. It would appear probable that the superstructure
covered not only the burial chamber but also the subsidiary
graves, and its over-all measurement would be approximately
29.2 by 20.8 metres. A great stela of black quartzose stone

Fig. 46.
Horus name
of Semerk-
het

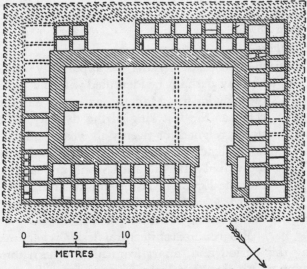

0   5   10
METRES

Fig. 47. Plan of Tomb U at Abydos

bearing the king's hawk name was found in the tomb (Fig. 48). On ivory tablets from Semerkhet's tomb there appears the name of a certain Henuka, whom we may judge to have been a senior official both during his reign and that of his successor (Fig. 49).

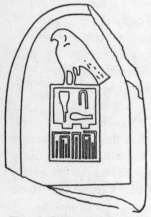

Fig. 48. Stela of Semerkhet from Abydos

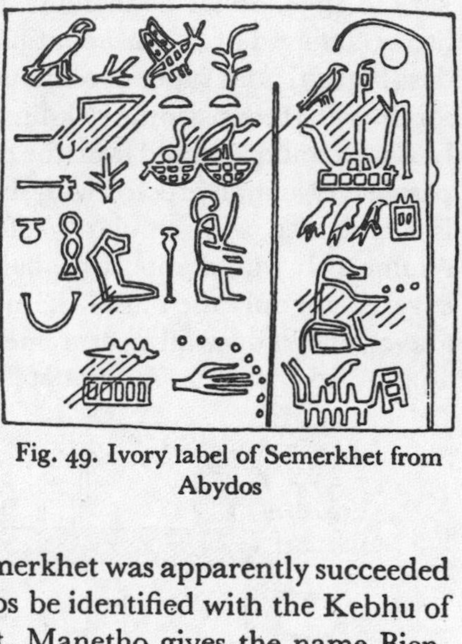

Fig. 49. Ivory label of Semerkhet from Abydos

Ka'a (*Figure 50*)

After his short reign, Semerkhet was apparently succeeded by Ka'a, who may perhaps be identified with the Kebhu of

Fig. 50.
Horus name
of Ka'a

the Abydos list. Manetho gives the name Bieneches as the last king of the dynasty, who, he states, reigned for twenty-six years; but there is no evidence to support any identification of this individual with Ka'a and it would appear possible that the Egyptian historian is at fault in at least the name, although he may have been correct in his recording of the length of the reign.

Progress in architectural design is very marked during this period and, apart from his southern tomb or cenotaph at Abydos, four large monuments of the reign of

Ka'a have been recently discovered at Sakkara, one of which, No. 3505, is almost certainly his actual burial place.

The king's tomb at Abydos (Fig. 51) is a more elaborate structure than those of his predecessors and the general design of the substructure corresponds closely with buildings of the same period at Sakkara. This consists of a deep rectangular pit with an entrance stairway descending from the north-west. On each side of the stairway are two magazines and both these and the burial chamber within the pit were originally roofed with timber. Surrounding the nucleus structure are more magazines and twenty-six subsidiary graves for retainers, all with higher floor levels than the burial chamber and stairway. There is reason to believe that the destroyed superstructure originally covered the whole tomb,

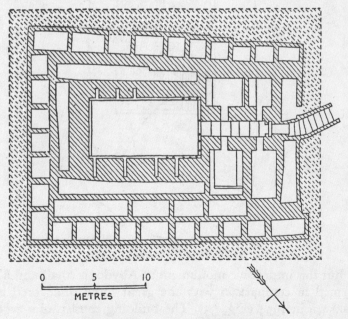

0   5   10

METRES

Fig. 51. Plan of Tomb Q at Abydos

measuring approximately 30 by 23 metres. Apart from jar-sealings and labels the monument can be identified by the discovery of the remains of two stelae on the east side of the structure, both of which bore his hawk name Ka'a (Fig. 52).

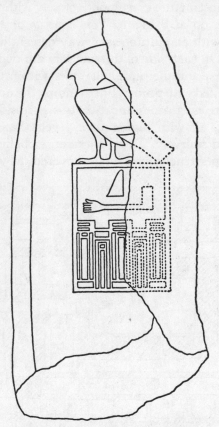

Fig. 52. Stela of Ka'a from Abydos

But this impressive monument at Abydos is small and ill-formed in comparison with the great tomb discovered at Sakkara in 1954 (Fig. 53). The building consists of a rect-angular brick superstructure with its exterior decorated with

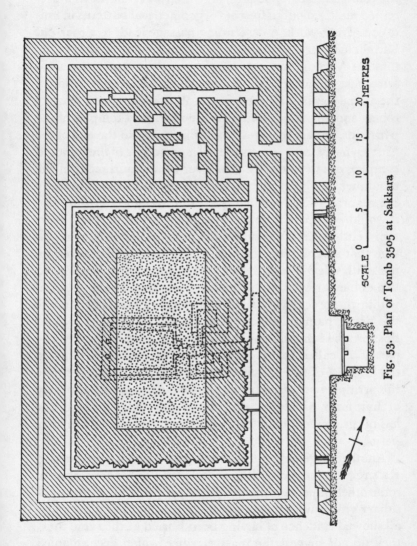

SCALE 0 5 10 15 20 METRES

Fig. 53. Plan of Tomb 3505 at Sakkara

the usual recessed panelling, on which were found well preserved multi-coloured frescoes of geometrical patterns in imitation of mat-work. A descending passage leads to a rock-cut
burial chamber and magazines of similar plan to that of the
tomb at Abydos. Surrounding the panelled superstructure is
a massive enclosure wall within which, on the north side of
the actual tomb, is a funerary temple consisting of a maze of
rooms and corridors similar to the mortuary temples of the
pyramids. In fact this great building, dated to the end of the
First Dynasty, may be considered a prototype of the pyramid
complex of later periods. The over-all measurement of the
monument is 65 by 37 metres. No traces of the subsidiary
burials of sacrificed retainers were found round the tomb and
it would appear that by the time of Ka'a this barbaric mortuary custom had died out in the more cultured North. It is
true that a subsidiary tomb of some size was discovered on
the south side of the entrance to the tomb, but this belonged
to a nobleman who was probably given the honour of burial
within the precincts of the royal burial place. The stela of
this noble, named Merka (Pl. 30a), was found near by and
this inscribed monument together with another smaller one
of a noble called Sabef, found in the Abydos tomb, show, in
the long list of titles inscribed on them, that in Ka'a's time
the writing had already developed well beyond a purely
archaic form. Moreover, the titles of these nobles are more or
less of the conventional form which became the rule in later
periods.

Another large tomb at Sakkara (No. 3500) is also dated to
Ka's reign, and may well have belonged to his consort or to
some other important member of the royal family. Four subsidiary graves were found adjoining this tomb, but although
all showed evidence of having been buried at the same time,
they do not suggest the mass sacrifice which accompanied
the burial of the kings at Abydos.

Apart from Merka and Sabef, the nobleman Henuka continued to hold office during the reign of Ka'a.

FIRST DYNASTY

Name	*Major monuments*
Hor-aha	Tomb B 19 at Abydos. (Petrie, *Royal Tombs*)
	Tomb 3357 at Sakkara. (Emery, *Hor-aha*)
	Tomb of Nithotep at Nagadeh. (de Morgan, *Recherches sur les origines de l'Égypte, Tombeau royal de Nagadeh.* Borchardt, 'Das Grab des Menes'. *Zeitschrift für ägyptische Sprache*, XXXVI)
Zer	Tomb O at Abydos. (Petrie, *Royal Tombs*)
	Tomb 3471 at Sakkara. (Emery, *Great Tombs*, I)
	Tomb 2185 at Sakkara. (Quibell, *Archaic Mastabas*)
Meryet-nit	Tomb Y at Abydos. (Petrie, *Royal Tombs*)
	Tomb 3503 at Sakkara. (Emery, *Great Tombs*, II)
	Enclosure of sacrifice burials. (Petrie, *Tombs of the Courtiers*)
Uadji	Tomb Z at Abydos. (Petrie, *Royal Tombs*)
	Tomb 3504 at Sakkara. (Emery, *Great Tombs*, II)
	Tomb at Gizeh. (Petrie, *Gizeh and Rifeh*)
Udimu	Tomb T at Abydos. (Petrie, *Royal Tombs*)
	Tomb 3035 at Sakkara. (Emery, *Tomb of Hemaka*)
	Tomb 3036 at Sakkara. (Emery, *Great Tombs*, I)
	Tomb 3506 at Sakkara. (Emery, *Great Tombs*, II)
Enezib	Tomb X at Abydos. (Petrie, *Royal Tombs*)
	Tomb 3038 at Sakkara. (Emery, *Great Tombs*, I)
Semerkhet	Tomb U at Abydos. (Petrie, *Royal Tombs*)
Ka'a	Tomb Q at Abydos. (Petrie, *Royal Tombs*)
	Tomb 3505 at Sakkara. (Emery; *Great Tombs*, III)
	Tomb 3500 at Sakkara. (Emery, *Great Tombs*, III)

THE SECOND DYNASTY

Hotepsekhemui (Figure 54)
The cause of the downfall of the First Dynasty is not known and the distinction between the two royal houses is not apparent. Manetho records that both were Thinite in origin but

their southern tombs – with the exception of those of Kha-sekhemui and Perabsen – if they existed, have not been found in this area and certainly they did not form part of the Abydos group at Um-el-Qu'ab. We may therefore conclude that Manetho's statement of a change of dynasty lies on a firm foundation. He tells us that the dynasty consisted of nine rulers who ruled for a total of 302 years. Of these kings, the order of succession of the first four is estab-lished on archaeological evidence, but after this the order and identification are very uncertain.

Fig. 54.
Horus name
of Hotep-
sekhemui

The founder of the dynasty was a king with the Horus name of Hotepsekhemui, who can be identified with Buzau of the king lists and the Boêthos of Manetho. His name Hotepsekhemui appears with those of his two immediate successors on a granite statue found at Memphis. It has been suggested on the evidence of a flint bowl found at Giza, that the order of the names on the statue is not necessarily chronolog-ical, but this is unlikely, and the sequence would appear to be correct. His tomb has not yet been found, but, judging from the discovery in a subterranean gallery near the pyramid of Unas at Sakkara of clay jar-sealings bearing his name, it would appear probable that his funerary monument was located in this area. Manetho records that, during this reign of thirty-eight years, a chasm opened at Bubastis and many people perished; as this area of the western Delta shows geological evidence of volcanic disturbance, the story probably has some foundation in fact.

Ra-neb (*Figure 55*)

Hotepsekhemui was succeeded by Ra-neb who is to be identified with Kakau of the king lists and Kaichos of Man-etho. His tomb has not been found, but as with his predecessor Hotepsekhemui, clay sealings belonging to him have been recovered from the subterranean galleries near the pyramid of Unas at Sakkara, so that his tomb is probably somewhere in this area. In the vicinity of an ancient trade route to the western oasis behind Armant, Ra-neb's name has been found crudely inscribed on the rocks (Fig. 56).

Manetho records that, during the reign of Ra-neb, the worship of the bulls of Apis at Memphis and of Mnevis at Heliopolis and the goat of Mendes were established; but as we have seen, the worship of Apis was already in existence during the First Dynasty. According to the Egyptian historian, Ra-neb reigned for thirty-nine years.

Fig. 55. Horus name of Ra-neb

Fig. 56. Rock-cut name of Ra-neb

Neteren (Netermu, Figure 57)

Neteren, the successor of Ra-neb, can be identified with Banentiru of the king lists and with Binôthris of Manetho, who states that he reigned for forty-seven years. Chronicles of the sixth to the twentieth years of the reign are preserved on the Palermo Stone, but they are not of great interest, being principally confined to religious feasts and the usual census figures. However, they do record the foundation of a palace or other important building called Hor-ren in the year 7, and, what is more important, indications of civil war in the year 13. Here reference is made to the destruction of Shemra and Ha ('House of the North'). The chronicles also record the 'running of Apis' in the years 9 and 15.

Fig. 57. Horus name of Neteren

According to Manetho, it was during the reign of Neteren that it was decided that women might occupy the throne;

which raises an important question in relation to the puzzling status of Queen Meryet-nit of the previous dynasty.

Neteren's tomb has apparently not been discovered yet. Jar-sealings bearing his name have been found in a tomb near Giza and the possibility must be envisaged that this was his burial place, although three large tombs at Sakkara can also be definitely dated to his reign, and one of immense size (2302, Fig. 58) might also be considered as his final resting

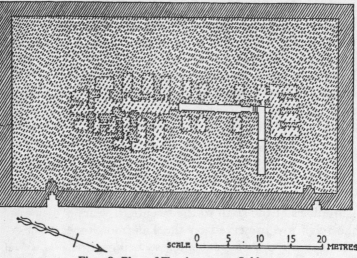

SCALE 0   5   10   15   20 METRES

Fig. 58. Plan of Tomb 2302 at Sakkara

place, even though the name of a noble called Ruaben was found on stone jar fragments discovered within the substructure of the building. The superstructure, measuring 58 by 32.64 metres, is built of brick with a solid, black mud filling. The exterior is plain with north and south chapels on the east side. A stairway descending from the east turns at right angles to the south and leads through a portcullis into a complicated series of rock-cut subterranean rooms. Sealings of Neteren have also been found in the vicinity of the pyramid of Unas at Sakkara. A small seated statuette of alabaster, in the Michailides Collection in Cairo, has been identified as that of Neteren from an inscription on the throne. The king, wearing the White Crown, is depicted in the conventional dress worn at the Sed festival.

Sekhemib (Figure 59)

Under Sekhemib, identified with Uaznes of the king list and Manetho's Tlas, some form of political and religious revolution took place. Although we cannot be certain, it would appear probable that the indigenous people of the Nile valley still occupied large areas of the land where they worshipped Set, the god-king of Egypt before the advent of the Followers of Horus. What political motives were behind Sekhemib's actions are unknown, but at some period of his short reign – seventeen years according to Manetho – he appears to have abandoned his allegiance to the god Horus and worshipped Set, changing his name to Perabsen, with the *serech* surmounted with the animal god Set instead of the Hawk which is above his original name of Sekhemib. Like Akhenaten of the Eighteenth Dynasty he erased his original name on his funerary stelae, already erected in his southern tomb at Abydos, and replaced it by his newly acquired Set name. Sekhemib's name with title 'Conqueror of the foreign lands' has been found on stone vase fragments from the Step Pyramid; but apart from this, no remains of his have been found at Sakkara. His only monument is represented by the tomb at Abydos (Fig. 60), which curiously enough is one of the group of the kings of the previous dynasty. The superstructure of the tomb has been entirely destroyed and only the brick-lined pit of the substructure, within which is a central burial chamber surrounded by magazines, remains. The structure is poorly built and even with its superstructure cannot have greatly exceeded an over-all measurement of 21 by 18.5 metres. An unusual feature is that the entrance is on the east side and it was near here that the two stelae, with their altered inscriptions, were discovered. No evidence has as yet been discovered which might explain the reversion to the worship of Set by a monarch of the Thinite dynasty, but the attitude of Sekhemib Perabsen is clearly shown by his alteration of name on his funerary stelae at Abydos, the figures of Set above his name of Perabsen on many seals, and above all

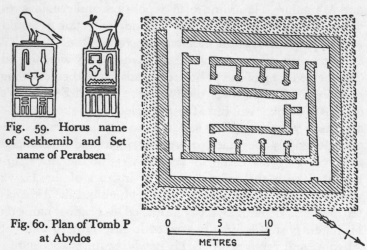

Fig. 59. Horus name of Sekhemib and Set name of Perabsen

Fig. 60. Plan of Tomb P at Abydos

on the seal of one of his nobles found in his tomb which reads 'The god of Ombos' (the centre of the Set tribes in Upper Egypt) 'to his son Perabsen'. It is possible that the Followers of Set, representing the indigenes, had increased in power to such an extent during the decline of Thinite power that the king found it sound policy to adopt the worship of their god, and certainly even his more powerful descendant Khasekhemui found it necessary to have the figure of Set in equality with Horus above his name. Our knowledge of the period is so fragmentary that it is impossible to postulate any hypothesis which would fit in with all the facts, but it appears almost certain that in Sekhemib's reign some form of religious revolution and a weakening of the rule of the Thinite kings took place. An archaeological fact which may have its explanation in the events of this undoubtedly disturbed period is the burning of the royal tombs. Nearly all the royal monuments at Abydos, Nagadeh, and Sakkara have been found badly damaged by fire and it was at first thought that this was the work of the early plunderers who wished to obliterate all signs of their sacrilege. However, recent excavation at Sakkara has yielded evidence which strongly suggests that this incendiarism was deliberately done with official sanction and perhaps we have here the results of the warring factions seeking to destroy the after-life of their dynastic opponents. The destruction by fire of these monuments certainly took place at an early date and we may not be in error in ascribing it to this period of obvious religious and political upheaval.

Whatever the results of the changes in his religious allegiance, Sekhemib's spirit was venerated and his cult was preserved at Memphis as well as that of his immediate successor Sendji, as late as the Fourth Dynasty.

Sendji

There are no contemporary monuments of Sendji, who was apparently Sekhemib's successor and is probably to be identified with Manetho's Sethenês whom he states reigned for forty-one years. Although so little is known at present concerning Sendji, it is evident that apart from his long reign he was a monarch of importance and we know that his cult was preserved until a late period; indeed a bronze statue bearing his name was made in the Twenty-Sixth Dynasty, more than 2000 years after his death.

Neterka

The sixth king of the dynasty, according to Manetho, was Chairês, who reigned seventeen years. No contemporary documents which might be attributed to him have been found, but according to the Turin king list, Sendji was succeeded by a certain Neterka and, although neither the Sakkara or Abydos lists mention him, it is possible that Neterka and Chairês were the same person.

Neferkara

According to Manetho, Chairês was succeeded by Nephercherês, who may be identified with Neferkara whose name appears on the Abydos king list. The Egyptian historian relates that he ruled for twenty-five years and that there is a legend that during his reign the Nile flowed with honey for eleven days.

Kha-sekhem (Figure 61)

The Second Dynasty ends with two kings: Kha-sekhem and Kha-sekhemui; some authorities believe both to be the same person, the former name being an earlier version of the latter adopted by the king when he had reunited Egypt after the religious wars which had split the country (i.e. 'appearance of the Two Powers' instead of 'appearance of the Power'). But on balance it would appear that Kha-sekhem and Kha-sekhemui were two persons, probably the eighth and ninth kings of the dynasty.

Fig. 61. Horus name of Kha-sekhem

Kha-sekhem would thus be identical with Huzefa (Neferka-sokar?) of the Sakkara and Turin lists and with Manetho's Sesôchris, who he states reigned for forty-eight years. Although this king's name is omitted on the Abydos list, there is little doubt that his control extended over the whole of Egypt, for monuments of his have been found at Hieraconpolis. But his reign appears to have been stormy and the only relics of the period, two statues, a stela, and three stone vessels, record war and conquest; and although some of these events may have occurred beyond Egypt's frontier, they indicate a period of national disturbance. The two statues, one of schist (Pl. 31) and one of limestone, are of exceptional artistic merit and they represent Kha-sekhem seated on a throne, wearing the crown of Upper Egypt and the robe usually associated with the Sed festival. Around the bases of both statues is a row of contorted human figures representing slain enemies and on the front is inscribed 'Northern enemies 47,209' (Fig. 62). It has been suggested

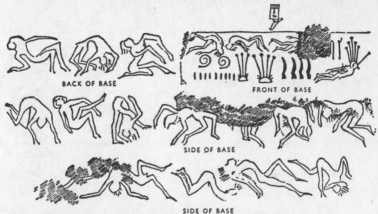

Fig. 62. Inscriptions on the base of the Kha-sekhem statues

that the 'northern enemies' were Libyans who had invaded the Delta, but we must not overlook the possibility of internal insurrection in Lower Egypt.

Further evidence of rebellion in the north comes from the three stone vessels which are identically inscribed 'The year of fighting the northern enemy within the city of Nekheb'. The goddess Nekhbet in vulture form holds a 'signet circle' within which is the word *besh* (rebels), while with the other claw she supports the emblem of the unity of Egypt before the name of Kha-sekhem (Fig. 63).

The fragment of the stela shows part of a kneeling captive, on a platform which ends in the head of a foreigner on which rests a bow (Fig. 64). Below is the name of Kha-sekhem and

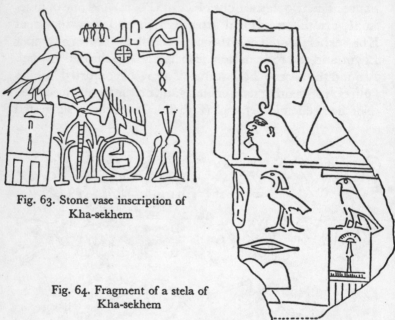

Fig. 63. Stone vase inscription of Kha-sekhem

Fig. 64. Fragment of a stela of Kha-sekhem

the text 'humbling the foreign lands'. It is important to note that on his statues the king is shown wearing only the White Crown of Upper Egypt and on the stone vases the hawk above his name also wears the White Crown. The impression gained from this admittedly limited evidence is that Kha-sekhem was a ruler of the Thinite family of Upper Egypt who restored the unity of the Nile valley after the religious wars between the followers of Horus and Set which had probably divided the country since the reign of Perabsen. His very name 'Appearance of the Power' is significant, and the absence of any contemporary monument of his at Sakkara strongly suggests that his rule was centred in the far south, for even at Abydos no trace of him has been discovered. All the objects described above were found at Hieraconpolis, the original capital of the followers of Horus. His tomb has not yet been discovered and he was perhaps buried in this area.

Assuming Kha-sekhem's identity with Manetho's eighth king, he must indeed have been a leader, for the Egyptian historian records that Sesôchris was 5 cubits and 3 palms high, which would make him a giant of about 8 feet!

Kha-sekhemui (Figure 65)

Kha-sekhem was succeeded by Kha-sekhemui, who was perhaps the most outstanding monarch of the dynasty, for under him the final unity of the country was established and the foundation laid for the astonishing expansion and development of Pharaonic power in the Third Dynasty. As ninth king of the Second Dynasty, he is to be identified with Zazai of the king lists and Chenerês of Manetho, who attributes to him a reign of thirty years.

The struggle between the followers of Horus and Set had come to an end and his name Kha-sekhemui, 'The appearance of the Two Powers', is added to by his fuller name 'The Two Gods in him are at peace'. On the numerous jar-sealings,

Fig. 65.
Horus-Set
name of
Kha-sek-
hemui

the king's Ka name is always surmounted by the hawk and the Set animal, a further indication that some form of unity on equal terms had been achieved.

The southern tomb of Kha-sekhemui at Abydos is a fantastic construction bearing no resemblance to other monuments on that site, or indeed to any other contemporary building at Sakkara (Fig. 66). Unfortunately, as with the other Abydos monuments, no superstructure remains, and we have only the substructure to judge of the immense size of the building. It measures 68.97 metres in length, with a

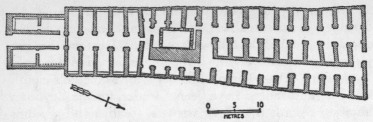

Fig. 66. Plan of Tomb V at Abydos

varying width of between 17.6 and 10.4 metres. It consists of three parts; at the north is a door leading to three rows of thirty-three magazines for offerings and funerary equipment; then comes a stone-built burial chamber flanked by four rooms on either side, and then a further ten magazines, five on each side of a corridor leading to the south door, which is flanked by four more rooms.

The burial chamber was at one time believed to be the oldest example of stone masonry in existence, but excavation at Sakkara and Helwan has shown that building in stone was known in the First Dynasty. A curious feature of Kha-sekhemui's tomb is its irregularity and faulty planning and, impressive as it is in size, it is difficult to believe that only a few years separate it from the magnificent Step Pyramid of Zoser at Sakkara. Apart from the remains of funerary equipment, such as stone and copper vessels, flint and copper tools, pottery, and basketwork, the king's sceptre of gold and sard was recovered from the tomb.

Kha-sekhemui also conducted building operations at Hierakonpolis, where a granite door jamb was recovered. This monument, bearing the double name of the king surmounted by Horus and Set, probably came from a temple long since destroyed. The workmanship is well advanced and the resemblance in style and execution to the sculptured work of the early Third Dynasty is so obvious that its date, at the end of the Second Dynasty, cannot be questioned. On the back of the jamb is a partly defaced inscription which depicts the king and the goddess Sheshet in what is obviously a foundation ceremony. Like his predecessor of the early First Dynasty, Kha-sekhemui appears to have adopted the political strategy of marriage with a northern princess, and his queen seems to have been Nemathap who, according to a jar-sealing from Abydos, bore the title of 'the king-bearing mother' (Fig. 67). She was later worshipped as the ancestress of the kings of the Third Dynasty.

Fig. 67. Jar-sealing of Queen Nemathap

With the death of Kha-sekhemui the Archaic Period of Egypt's history comes to an end, and the united Two Lands stand on the threshold of the glorious epoch of the pyramid builders.

SECOND DYNASTY

Name	*Major monuments*
Hotepsekhemui	Tomb unknown. Jar-sealings from Sakkara (Barsanti, 'Fouilles autour de la Pyramide d'Ounas', *Annales du Service des Antiquités*, vol. III, p. 182)
Ra-neb	Tomb unknown
Neteren	Tomb unknown. Tomb of Ruaben. No. 2302 at Sakkara. (Quibell, *Archaic Mastabas*)
Sekhemib-Perabsen	Tomb P at Abydos. (Petrie, *Royal Tombs*)
Sendji	No contemporary monuments
Neterka	No contemporary monuments
Neferkara	No contemporary monuments

Kha-sekhem	Tomb unknown. Statues and stela from Hieraconpolis. (Quibell, *Hierakonpolis*)
Kha-sekhemui	Tomb V at Abydos. (Petrie, *Royal Tombs*) Temple remains from Hieraconpolis. (Quibell, *Hierakonpolis*)

Chapter 2

THE STATE

THE MONARCHY

THE monarchy of Egypt's first two dynasties appears to have had all the characteristics which we associate with later periods. It was absolute, and the king was a god incarnate, and, although there were naturally distinctions of class there were no castes, for all were commoners before the 'good god' who was identified with Horus. Well may we accept the question and answer of the Vizier Rekhmire, written about 1500 B.C., as being as true of the monarchy during the Archaic Period as it was during the Empire, nearly 1700 years later. Rekhmire wrote:

What is the King of Upper and Lower Egypt? He is a god by whose dealings one lives, the father and mother of all men, alone by himself, without an equal.

But it was a dual monarchy and, so soon after the unification, the individuality of two states of the North and South was more marked than in later times. In fact there appear to have been two separate administrations united only under the throne. Even the elaborate ceremonies of the king's coronation, his 'Sed' festival or jubilee and ultimate burial, were twice repeated with the different insignia, architecture, and customs of Upper and Lower Egypt.

The insignia of royalty of the two lands were at first separate and the kings are shown sometimes wearing the White Crown (Hedjet) of the South and sometimes the Red Crown (Deshert) of the North. But soon, some long-forgotten designer produced the 'Double Crown' (Sekhemti), a combination of the two emblems, and henceforth, except when the monarch was specifically portrayed as the ruler of one or other of the two lands, he is shown wearing the crown of all Egypt (Fig. 68).

Fig. 68. The White, Red, and Double Crowns of Egypt

Throughout Egypt's long history the royal titulary shows plainly that the conception of two distinct and separate nations united under one monarch was strictly adhered to, and indeed even to this day the distinction between the two lands survives in many ways. The titulary of the kings of the Archaic Period appears to have been confined to three of the five 'great names' in common use during later times. First we have the 'Horus name' which was written inside a rect-angular frame representing the 'Great House' or royal palace with its recessed panelling, reproductions of which we have in the superstructure of the northern tombs at Sakkara (Fig. 69A). Surmounting this rectangular frame (known as the *serekh*) is the falcon of Horus, the dynastic god of all Egypt (identified with the sun god and the son and avenger of Osi-ris, the symbol of dead kingship). This, the Horus name, took precedence on the monuments over all other names and is the only certain identification found on objects discovered at Abydos and Sakkara.

No surer indication of a change in loyalties is shown than when we find the Set animal above the *serekh* of Perabsen in the Second Dynasty, for in this, his first name, this king identified himself with the deity whom he believed to be supreme throughout Egypt.

Second comes the *nebti* name, so called because of the reading of the preliminary title 'The Two Ladies', represented by figures of the vulture of the goddess Nekhbet of Upper Egypt and the cobra of the goddess Wadjet of Lower Egypt (Fig. 69B). This title above the second name of the king symbolizes the fact that he is the force uniting the dual monarchy of the Nile valley. The *nebti* name goes back at least to the time of Hor-aha at the commencement of the First Dynasty.

The third name which was taken by the king at his assumption of power was preceded by the title *nesu-bit* (Fig. 69c), meaning 'He who belongs to the sedge and bee'. We do not yet know the exact meaning of these two symbols but the sedge sign certainly represented Upper Egypt and the bee Lower Egypt, and the meaning is clear: it represents the title 'King of Upper and Lower Egypt'. The *nesu-bit* name first appears on objects of King Udimu, but this does not necessarily mean that it was not in use at an earlier period.

It is the various names that each king bore which have caused such confusion in their identification, for whereas the all-important Horus name predominates on objects from their contemporary monuments, the king lists of the Eighteenth Dynasty use their *nesu-bit* names and Manetho appears to have used the Grecianized form of either the *nesu-bit* or the *nebti* names. It is only occasionally that

Fig. 69.
The 'Three Great Names'

on contemporary monuments we find the Horus, *nebti*, and *nesu-bit* names in correlation.

The king was a being apart and as the living Horus was the link between gods and men; as such he must not be allowed to fail either from age or ill health. It would appear probable that in primitive times, when the king showed signs of failing powers, he was forcibly removed by death. But this was in the dim and distant past, and by the time of the Unification, priestly magic had replaced barbaric custom and instead of violent replacement, the king's vigour was revived by the mysterious ceremonies of the Sed festival. Although the festival appears to have had the character of a jubilee and a reassertion of the king's sovereignty and possession of the land of Egypt, it was certainly more than a mere commemoration of the royal accession. It was a necessary rejuvenation of the king, for as Rekhmire tells us, the king 'is a god by whose dealings one lives' and thus the whole nation was deeply concerned with the celebration of these important rites. Sometimes the festival took place thirty years after the king's assumption of power, but judging from the evidence of the Palermo Stone, the Sed festival was celebrated by some of the archaic kings repeatedly and at much shorter intervals. Our knowledge of the actual ceremonial of the feast is uncertain, but some features can be interpreted with reasonable clearness.

In order to celebrate the festival, special buildings were erected, which included a Throne Room and a Robing Room in which the king changed his dress and insignia according to the various double rites connected with the two lands. But most important was the Heb-Sed Court, flanked on both sides with chapels of the Upper and Lower Egyptian gods of each nome or province. It would appear that in the open space between the two rows of shrines, the king, attired alternately in the insignia of Upper and Lower Egypt, ran a ritual race round a course which was called the 'field'. The king ran round the boundaries of the 'field' four times as the ruler of the South and four times as ruler of the North. Probably the 'field' represented Egypt and the ritual race perhaps signified his claim as possessor of the land; also, as the source of the national fertility, his action made the land fruitful and productive.

Other ceremonies took place during the Sed festival, such as the act of homage to the king by the 'Great Ones of Upper and Lower Egypt'; but the actual act of the rejuvenation of the monarch is not, as yet, understood; neither is the meaning of Heb-Sed, the name of the feast. But undoubtedly further research on this vital subject will reveal ultimately the basic foundation of the Egyptians' conception of kingship.

THE GOVERNMENT

Like the monarchy, the actual government of the united country was dual, and we find that the two nations had each their own centre of administration consisting of chancellery and treasury, housed in the 'White House' of the South and the 'Red House' of the North. In later times, the dual character of Egypt's government more or less disappeared; but during the period of the first two dynasties it undoubtedly existed. Indeed from the limited evidence it would appear that there were two viziers, one for Upper Egypt and one for Lower Egypt, and it seems evident that the only semblance of union for the two administrations was in the person of the king.

Each of the two lands was divided into 'nomes' or provinces, which were survivals of the tribal areas of the Predynastic period. The governors of these provinces were, perhaps, at that early period descendants of the earlier tribal chiefs and were the 'great ones' who advised the king.

From jar-sealings and inscribed labels we can see that there was an effective fiscal organization, central control of the irrigation of the Nile, an organized judicial system, and all the indications of an effective administrative machinery. We even find the title 'Scribe of Secrets', which might suggest the existence of that necessity of the modern world, a security service!

THE SOCIAL CLASSES

Through the evidence obtained from their burial customs, we are able to distinguish three distinct social classes in Egypt during the period of the first two dynasties. These groups consist of the nobility, officials and artisans, and the peasantry. Burial grounds of each of these three main ranks of the population are well represented in the districts surrounding Menes' capital, the 'White Wall' (Memphis). Behind the city at Sakkara we have what appear to be the tombs of the kings, members of the royal family, and the great nobles, equipped with all the furniture and necessities of a highly civilized and luxurious way of life. Across the river at Helwan are the tombs of the lesser nobility and official classes, similar in design. Although much smaller and with less valuable equipment, they too show a high standard of living. The artisan class is, as yet, only represented in the subsidiary graves which surround the tombs of the kings and great nobles. But here again we find funerary structures which are miniature copies of those of their masters, and the carefully coffined bodies were surrounded with food and drink and the equipment necessary to their various crafts.

So much for the rulers of the land and their immediate followers and subordinates, all of whom appear to form a group apart, ruling and controlling the mass of the people who, during the period of the First Dynasty, were probably in the main racially separate, being descendants of the indigenous inhabitants of the Nile valley before the advent of the dynastic race. Their graves, well represented throughout Egypt, are just a natural development of the late predynastic burial. With the exception of the larger graves of the village notables, the burials, with their shallow pits and circular superstructure, are not rich in equipment, and, in comparison with the graves of the sacrificed retainers and artisans of the nobility, are poor and bear all the marks of a serf people. But towards the end of the Second Dynasty the results of racial fusion become apparent and there is evidence that the lower orders in many parts of the country adopted the burial customs of their superiors, a fact which in all probability was reflected in their everyday life.

Although the records are, as yet, too meagre to make any certain analysis of the social system of that remote period, the general indications are that it was mainly feudal in character: a large serf population of the indigenes serving a nobility of superior race and culture. The mass of this serf people would be employed in agriculture, but a proportion must have served in the mines and quarries, the construction of irrigation projects, military service, and the building of temples, palaces and tombs. Gradually they would come into closer contact with their rulers by the growth of an artisan class, which, towards the close of the Archaic Period, must have caused the fusion of races. This in later times was to develop into the all-important middle class, so essential and powerful in the Pharaonic state.

Chapter 3

THE MILITARY SYSTEM

AT a period such as this the military formed an important section of the community; but recruited, as they must have been, from all social levels of the master race, they cannot be distinguished as a class. In the formative years following the Unification, it is probable that the warriors were exclusively the descendants of the dynastic race; but as the pacification of the land progressed and the Pharaonic power became established, recruitment for the army would be extended to the mass of the indigenous population.

ORGANIZATION

In later times the army was organized on a feudal system, and we have every reason to believe that this system must have originated in the Archaic Period. As the power of the early Thinite kings extended, the conquered tribal chiefs would be compelled to supply their overlord with soldiers and so the system would grow and each province or nome would send its young men to serve the king under their own tribal standard and probably led by their own headman. We have no knowledge of any officer class or indeed of the system of leadership, but over-all control of the armies apart from that of the king must certainly have existed.

EQUIPMENT

Let us examine the equipment of these early warriors. They appear to have had no body armour, neither did they carry a shield. Their weapons consisted of the bow and arrow, the spear, the axe, the mace, and the dagger. The bow was small, not exceeding 3 ft in length, and shaped in the form shown in Fig. 70. Unfortunately, no wooden bows of the period have

Fig. 70. Archaic warriors from the 'Hunter's palette'

as yet been found and we are dependent for our knowledge of the design from figures on late predynastic palettes. But with regard to arrows, we are more fortunate, for hundreds of specimens of varied types were found in the remains of leather quivers in one of the great tombs at Sakkara. The size and lightness of these arrows confirms the comparative smallness of the bow, which can only otherwise be estimated by the portrayal of it on the palettes. The five types of arrows shown in Fig. 71 were apparently in common use. The first type has an average length of $19\frac{1}{2}$ in. and has a head formed by an agate lunate cemented to the top of a short ebony stick which is socketed into a hollow reed shaft. The base of the shaft has two feathers attached with gum and thread, and has a V-shaped notch for the bowstring. This type of arrow with its lunate head continued to be used in Egypt until at least as late as the Eighteenth Dynasty. The second type also has a lunate head of agate but smaller in size and attached to an ivory stick socketed into the reed shaft which also has feathers at the base, but with a square-cut notch instead of the V-cut for the bowstring. The third type has a barbed head formed by the jaw of a small fish cemented on to an ivory stick. The reed shaft is feathered, with a square-cut

notch. The fourth and fifth types differ only in the size of the
head, which is just a plain ivory point socketed direct into
the reed shaft. Arrows of these two types are not feathered,
as it was only considered necessary for those with the ill-
balanced heads of the first, second, and third types. It is interesting to note that arrows of the third and fifth types have
the tips of their heads painted red, either to denote that they

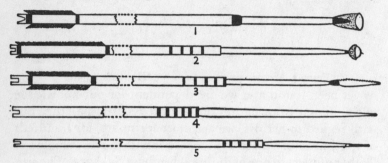

Fig. 71. Types of arrows

were poisoned or with the idea of sympathetic magic which
would draw the arrow to the blood of the target. Flint-
headed arrows of a heavier type were also very common.

Stabbing spears with copper and ivory heads have been
found, but these probably represent the superior weapons of
the nobility and we may conclude that flint-headed spears
would be in common use by the rank and file.

The short-hafted battle-axe with both stone and copper
blade was also in common use. The head was attached to the
haft with leather thongs. We have the figure of a warrior on
one of the late predynastic palettes which shows him carry-
ing a battle-axe with a double head; but no weapon of this
type has actually been found.

The mace with short haft and stone head of two types was
a favourite weapon. The most common type of head was
pear-shaped, as shown in Figs. 72 and 73B, and in scenes of

the king ceremonially killing his defeated enemy he is almost invariably shown to be armed with this weapon (Fig. 4). Great ceremonial mace-heads of the pear-shaped type engraved with scenes of historical importance were kept in the temples. The second type, shown in Fig. 73A, was obviously a light weapon, probably with a short haft, for combat at close quarters.

Daggers had blades of both flint and copper, with handles of wood, bone, or ivory. The weapon was carried in the belt.

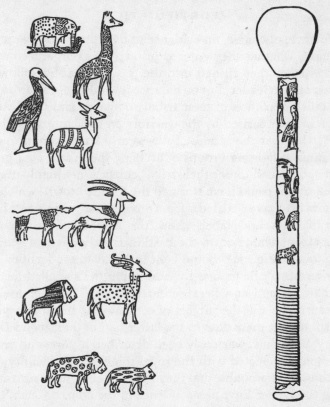

Fig. 72. Gold mace-handle with stone mace-head, from Nubia

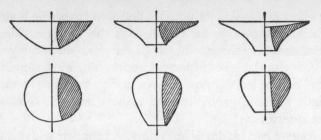

Fig. 73. Types of stone mace-heads

FORTIFICATION

We have, of course, no evidence of how these early warriors fought, whether they entered into battle as organized units or whether they rushed into the fray as a rabble following their chosen leader. But on balance it would appear, from the detailed depiction of their tribal standards and the distinction in arms carried by the warriors on the Hunter's palette (Pl. 1b), that the armies of these early kings were properly organized fighting groups of archers, spearmen, etc., properly controlled under their tribal chiefs. Only highly organized troops could have stormed the fortified towns which we know to have existed, for conventional representations on palettes and labels show the symbolical falcon and his allies hacking down the bastioned walls of enemy camps or towns (Fig. 74). Some conception of these fortified enclosures may be gained by examining the so-called forts of Kha-sekhemui and Perabsen at Abydos. The immense enclosures are still the subject of controversy, but it is beyond dispute that these date to the latter half of the Second Dynasty. They have variously been described as forts and valley temples connected with the royal tombs in the vicinity, but I consider it probable that they were the enclosures surrounding the Upper Egyptian residence of the king. As such, they were built to give maximum protection to the monarch, and although they cannot be described as forts they embodied unmistakable features of military architecture. The structure ascribed to Kha-sekhemui, from the evidence of jar-sealings, is rectangular in plan, with double walls separated by a corridor. The over-all measurement of the enclosure is 465 ft from north to south and 250 ft from east to west; the outer wall is 11 ft thick and the inner and main wall 18 ft thick, standing probably to a minimum height of 30 ft. There were four gateways and the two principal ones situated in the north-east and south-east corners are designed on sound military principles of defence (Figs. 75 and 76). The enclosure of Perabsen is smaller and has only one wall, but the surviving gateway shows the same principle of defence. Another great enclosure of similar type exists at Hieraconpolis, and although no definite dating evidence has been found, it would appear probable that the structure also belongs to the Archaic Period.

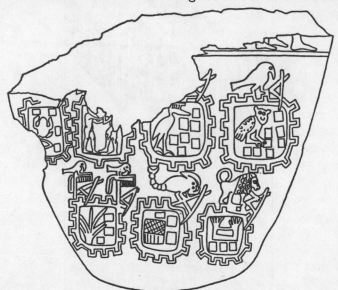

Fig. 74. Fragment of a stone palette, showing fortified enclosures

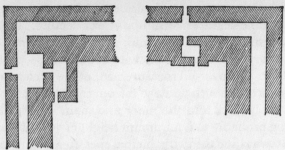

Fig. 75. Plan of fortified gateways

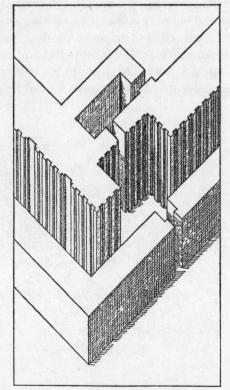

Fig. 76. Axonometric view of fortified gateway

Chapter 4

RELIGION

THE GODS

WITH the paucity of written material our knowledge of religion in Archaic Egypt is necessarily limited, but as the work of research progresses we are able to identify more and more of the gods who were well known in later periods as having been worshipped by the Egyptians of the earliest times.

Prior to the Unification there was a multitude of cults unconnected and entirely localized, each being the particular worship of the god of the tribe. The evolution of these cults was part of the political development of Egypt, for as the tribal areas became welded into principalities and finally into the two separate kingdoms of the North and South, so a mythology was created which united the tribal deities. The god of the conquered tribe was not suppressed but was annexed by the conqueror, who supplanted his defeated predecessor as a son of the deity. These tribal gods became the 'nome' gods of later times and their prerogatives were maintained by the king, who claimed their special protection, just as in prehistoric times had some long-forgotten chieftain.

By the time of the Unification we find the tribes of the dynastic race, both in the North and South, worshipping as their supreme deity the sky-god Horus whose symbol was the falcon, while the descendants of the indigenes appear to have acknowledged Set as their chief god. In early times, these Set-worshipping people were a very powerful section of the population of the Nile valley, occupying a large area of Upper Egypt centred round Ombos (in the modern province of Keneh). So powerful were they that at one time their god Set became the equal of Horus and indeed, at one period during the Second Dynasty, Set displaces Horus as the royal deity. An echo of the struggle between the Horus and Set worshippers is contained in the myths of later times relating to the triumph of good, represented by Horus, over evil, represented by Set.

We know nothing of the origin of Horus, but certainly by the time of the Unification he may be recognized as a sky-god, and the religion of the king who was the living Horus was undoubtedly a celestial cult, just as it was in later times. Prior to recent discoveries at Sakkara it was generally believed that Sun worship only became the religion of the state during the Pyramid Age, but the existence of the graves of funerary barks attached to the big tombs at Sakkara and later found with the burials of the nobility at Helwan show that the primary belief that the dead must join the company of the gods on their journey across the heavens was generally accepted, even as early as the commencement of the First Dynasty. Other gods of the dynastic people, mostly local and tribal in origin, were soon absorbed into the circle of sky mythology, but the mass of the population descended from the indigenes who in the early years of the dual monarchy, forming a distinct and largely separate racial group, still gave their allegiance to the tribal gods of their ancestors, and above all to Set. As the fusion of the two main racial groups progressed under the stable influence of the united control of the two lands, many of these ancient gods were assimilated into the solar synthesis and their primitive characteristics were obliterated. But Set was not assimilated and throughout Egyptian history he remains a deity apart, for because of political reasons in the Archaic Period, his cult was a rallying point for the dispersed people of predynastic Egypt. His existence could not be ignored, but except at certain short periods, and obviously on grounds of political expediency, Set was considered to be the personification of evil; so much so that in Classical times he was identified with Typhon. But in the period with which we deal, Set probably was the beneficent deity of a large proportion of the inhabitants of the Nile valley long before he became a part of the Osirian synthesis of which I will write later. Set was represented by an unidentified animal which had the appearance of a dog with a vertical tail with a split tip, and the head of an ant-eater with high square-topped ears.

Thus, in early dynastic Egypt there were two distinct and irreconcilable cults, which only became temporarily united at the close of the Second Dynasty as a matter of political expediency. But there were other major religions, notably Rē at Heliopolis, Ptah at Memphis, Osiris at Busiris, and Min of Coptos, which although gradually recast in some form of theoretical unity, must, so soon after the Unification, have remained largely distinct. Indeed a reasonable unity was never really attained and throughout Egyptian history the theologians never succeeded in forming a pantheon which was not riddled with inconsistencies.

The worship of the sun-god Rē seems to have originated at Heliopolis, which remained the centre of his cult until the rise of Christianity. The god was conceived as the sun itself in the form of the disk. When the Thinite kings established the capital at Memphis, they perhaps came under the influence of the priesthood of the sun-cult which probably was firmly established long before the Unification. The ultimate result appears to have been a fusion of the sky-god Horus with the sun-god Rē, as a composite deity Rē-Harakhte and the king identified with Horus became the son of Rē. But this fusion seems not to have occurred until the Second Dynasty, although the symbol of the winged disk appears above the Horus name of Uadji on a comb found at Abydos (Fig. 146).

When Menes selected the site of his capital in an area near the apex of the Delta, a local god of the neighbourhood soon came into prominence. This was Ptah, who according to the Memphite theology was the creator of the universe. It is possible that the god originated in some long-forgotten human genius, for unlike the mass of Egyptian deities he was not represented in animal form or with any animal attributes. He is shown as a man wrapped in the garments of a mummy with no headdress but a close fitting skull cap.

The cult of Ptah remained powerful throughout Egyptian history, particularly with the educated classes, for unlike those of other gods it was predominantly spiritual and attained a higher level of religious thinking than that of the other more materialistic Egyptian faiths. Although Ptah has not been precisely identified in any contemporary documents, it is possible that the mummiform figure carried in processions on the label of Zer (Fig. 21) is a representation of him. Manetho tells us that Menes built a temple to Ptah at Memphis and the records of the First and Second Dynasties on the Palermo Stone mention the feast of Sokar, god of the Memphite necropolis, who was assimilated to Ptah.

Until recently it was questioned as to whether the worship of Osiris had developed in archaic times; but the discovery at Helwan of the *Dad* symbol of the god and the girdle tie of his female counterpart Isis (both of First Dynasty date) shows that the cult which was to remain the most favoured of the masses of Egypt throughout her long history was already in existence. The cult, although having characteristics of nature worship, was primarily the worship of dead kingship, and the myth of Osiris seems to be an echo of long-forgotten events which actually took place. These events were perhaps originally unconnected and belonged to different periods which were later welded together into a moral story of the struggle between good and evil. The myth of the treacherous murder of the good king Osiris by his brother Set, and the vengeance and re-establishment of beneficent rule by Osiris' son Horus who founded a line of demi-gods from whom the Pharaohs were descended all suggest episodes perhaps connected with the prehistoric struggles between the dynastic peoples and the indigenes of the Nile valley. At this stage of our knowledge it is idle to speculate, but the recent discovery at Helwan of proof of the existence of Osiris and Isis in the First Dynasty suggests that the connexion of the royal god Horus with Osiris, the symbol of dead kingship, was not entirely the result of the theological jugglery of later times but was perhaps based on some historical foundation.

The original centre of the Osiris cult was at Busiris in the eastern delta; but he was not the primitive god of this locality. He had supplanted a more ancient deity called Andjti, from whom he took certain features of his regalia, such as the double plumes of his crown and the shepherd's crook. We have no representation of Osiris in the Archaic Period but the seated mummiform figure of King Udimu on the label of Hemaka (Fig. 37) is an accurate forerunner of the appearance of the god as portrayed in later monuments; so much so that some authorities have mistaken the figure for that of Osiris, whereas it represents the king in the garments of the dead, at his Sed festival.

Other deities of lesser importance are known to have been worshipped in archaic times. Anubis, a god of the dead and a protector of the necropolis, was also an important figure in Osirian mythology, represented in early times as a seated wolf or dog. Feasts of Anubis are mentioned in the First Dynasty records on the Palermo Stone.

Aker, a cosmic god, was represented as the two fore-parts

of a lion joined together, each facing in opposite directions. Aker was supposed to guard the two horizons and the sun god entered the mouth of one lion in the evening and emerged out of the mouth of the other at dawn. In the religious literature of later periods, Aker is represented as two complete seated lions, back to back, and described as representing today and tomorrow.

Apis was the sacred bull of Memphis. Bull worship was well established long before the Unification and probably before the advent of the dynastic race. This animal symbolized for the Egyptians strength in war and in fertility, and as such was considered the abode of a supernatural power. Apis was a manifestation of the god Ptah and the Classical author Aelian tells us that the worship of this bull was established by Menes. Archaeological evidence tends to confirm this and certainly the cult was in existence during the First Dynasty. The early dynastic kings were frequently shown as bulls and it would appear that for political reasons they adopted the bull cult of the North, particularly Apis who perhaps existed long before the first king of united Egypt.

Harsaphes (Harishaf), a sacred ram, is mentioned in the First Dynasty records on the Palermo Stone. The cult of rams, like the bull worship, was common as early as the First Dynasty and probably for the same reason.

Hathor was a sky and cow goddess who in later times was considered to be the patron of love and joy and was represented as a cow, or woman with a cow's head, or with a human head having the horns and ears of a cow. But in early dynastic times, Hathor seems to have been a female counterpart of Horus, and even in later times her name meant 'House of Horus'. The earliest certain representation of her appears on the palette of Narmer, where she is shown with a human face and a cow's ears and horns.

Khent-Amentiu was a god of the dead at Abydos who was

assimilated with Osiris and in later times represented in a similar fashion.

Matit or Mehit was a lioness goddess of Hieraconpolis and Thinis. She is represented on numerous First Dynasty sealings as a recumbent lioness with three or four bent bars projecting from her back and invariably she is shown in front of a wicker-work shrine which in later times was the determinative sign for the 'Great House' or palace of the king.

Mefdet, a cat goddess, is mentioned in the First Dynasty records on the Palermo Stone. She is depicted in later times as a female figure clad in a cat's skin and was considered a protectress against snake bite.

Min was the tutelary god of travellers and the whole eastern desert was considered his domain. The centre of his worship was at Akhmim and Coptos at the western termination of the great trade route of the Wadi-el-Hammamat. He is represented ithyphallically in human form, wrapped as a mummy, with an upraised arm holding a whip, and wearing a head-dress of two tall plumes. Min was an indigenous deity of great antiquity and two statues of probably predynastic date were found at Coptos. These may be considered the oldest examples of large-scale sculpture in the Nile valley.

Nekhbet was the tutelary goddess of Hieraconpolis (Nek-heb, El Kab), and as the influence of the people from this centre spread by conquest she became the guardian deity of Upper Egypt. In later times she is often represented as a woman with a vulture head wearing the white crown, but in the Archaic Period she is always portrayed plainly as a vulture. Nekhbet was the first of the 'Two Ladies' of the *nebti* name of the kings (see page 107).

Nit was the goddess of Sais in the western delta. Her symbol was a shield and crossed arrows, in reference to her character as a hunting and war deity, and this symbol was used even at an early period prior to the Unification. In the period with which we deal, the worship of Nit was widespread and she was considered one of the principal deities of Lower Egypt. The oldest temple of which we have any direct evidence in the time of Hor-aha (Menes) is that of this goddess. There is reason to believe that the Thinite kings, in order to legitimize their claim to rule the North, married Lower Egyptian princesses; three of the earliest queens of whom we have knowledge have the name of Nit as part of their names of Nithotep, Meryet-nit, and Her-nit.

Sed is mentioned in the First Dynasty records on the Palermo Stone. He was a god of the dead and is perhaps to be identified with Wepwawet, for he is depicted in the same manner as a wolf standing on a 'nome' standard.

Seshat was a goddess of learning and in later times she was believed to record on the leaves of the 'Tree of Heaven' all the deeds and duration of men and gods. Seshat's symbol is a star on a pole surmounted by what appear to be inverted horns. Her worship goes back to the First Dynasty, when the 'stretching of the cord' or the measuring out of the ground plan of a temple by a priest of the goddess is recorded in the annals on the Palermo Stone. This symbolical planning of sacred buildings was apparently one of the functions of Seshat's priesthood.

Thot, a moon god and patron of the sciences, was apparently worshipped as early as the First Dynasty, for the baboon (cynocephalus) was one of his sacred animals in conjunction with Apis on two monuments dated to the reign of Udimu. The standard of Thot also appears on palettes of the Predynastic period and a shrine of this god certainly existed in the time of Narmer.

Wadjet was the cobra goddess of Buto and the guardian of Lower Egypt. She was the second of the 'Two Ladies' of the royal *nebti* name.

Wepwawet, 'Opener-of-ways', appears originally to have

been a war-god who led the king to battle, but in later times he became a god of the dead, and as such was assimilated to Anubis. He is depicted as a wolf standing on a nome-standard.

Most of the gods of the Archaic Period of whom we have cognisance are presented in animal or fetish form, but already in the Second Dynasty anthropomorphization was developing and we have examples of Horus and Set in human form but with bird and animal heads.

To sum up, even the limited amount of material at present available shows that very many of the gods well-known in later times were already in existence during the period of the first two dynasties. Their characteristics were perhaps different, as in many cases the process of assimilation was only in its early stages; but the main outline of the religious conceptions of a later age are already discernible. The two great cults of Rē and Osiris were already in rival development, side by side, and although the third great religion of Set was doomed to ultimate disfavour, in this early period it had a vast following. Efforts to rationalize the theologies were taking place, but the inconsistencies of which we have evidence in archaic times were never to be satisfactorily removed.

WORSHIP AND RITUAL

Of the method of worship and religious ritual we have no evidence, but it probably differed little from that of later ages with the service to the god performed by priests in the seclusion of the sanctuary and with the people excluded from the innermost parts of the temple. The people saw only the statue or fetish of the god when it was brought out in processions on the days of festival. Judging from the records on the Palermo Stone, the festivals of many gods were of considerable frequency and it is obvious that the observance of religion was just as important in the life of the newly united nation as it was in many hundreds of years of Egypt's history. Of the temples we have little knowledge beyond crude representations on labels and jar-sealings. They appear to have been rather primitive wooden structures, and such was the conservatism of the Egyptians that even at a time when they were capable of building such well-designed and balanced structures as the great tombs at Sakkara for the actual house of the god, they may have retained the ancient designs of their forefathers. Indeed the design of these ancient religious buildings survives in the structures which were the innermost sanctuaries of the temples of later times. It is probable that even in the Archaic Period the wooden house of the god as shown on the wooden label of Hor-aha, represented the actual shrine of Nit with perhaps a massive temple structure surrounding it.

BURIAL CUSTOMS

The burial customs of the master race of Archaic Egypt were, like their religious beliefs, fundamentally the same as those of their descendants of later times. But during the greater part of the period under review, the mass of the population descended from the indigenes followed the mortuary customs of their forebears, only adopting the methods of burial of their superiors towards the end of the Second Dynasty, and then only in the metropolitan areas where racial fusion had developed to a large extent.

Whatever his religious beliefs, the Egyptian firmly believed in life after death, and whether he travelled with the sun-god in the heavens or dwelt with Osiris in the underworld he believed that a certain vital part of him continued to exist in the neighbourhood of the body. The body must therefore be preserved so that this vital force could return to it and be sustained in every comfort by food and drink, furniture, games,

(a) Carved ivory handle of the
Gebel-el-Arak knife

(b) The Hunter's palette

(b) Funerary stela of Uadji

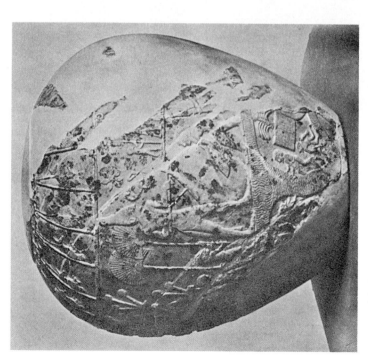

(a) Ceremonial mace head of the Scorpion King

2

(b) Fragment of a ceremonial palette

(a) Ceremonial palette of Narmer

3

East façade of the tomb of Queen Her-nit at Sakkara

West façade of the tomb of Queen Meryet-nit at Sakkara

5

East façade of Tomb 3506 at Sakkara

6

Painted decoration preserved on the façade of the tomb of Ka'a at Sakkara

Part of the bulls' heads bench of the east façade of the tomb of Uadji at Sakkara

The bulls' heads bench from above

Entrance stairway of a typical Second Dynasty tomb at Sakkara

Portcullis blocking before the burial chamber of a Second Dynasty tomb
at Sakkara

Clearing the filling of the interior of the superstructure of a Second Dynasty tomb which contained scattered groups of pottery

The interior of the superstructure after excavation with some of the pottery discovered in it

13

Stone flooring in the funerary temple of Ka'a at Sakkara

Timber roofing over the entrance stairway of Tomb 3506 at Sakkara

Portcullis blocking before the entrance of the burial chamber of Tomb
3035 at Sakkara

Stairway and stone built gate of Tomb 3506 at Sakkara

A First Dynasty boat grave partly buried beneath a Third Dynasty tomb at Sakkara

The model estate of Hor-aha at Sakkara

Wine jars stored in one of the substructure magazines of a First Dynasty
tomb at Sakkara

Wooden flooring of the burial chamber of a First Dynasty tomb at Sakkara

A subsidiary burial of the early First Dynasty

22

Subsidiary burial of the early First Dynasty, containing the skeleton of a dwarf

(a) Wooden coffin for a contracted burial, Second Dynasty

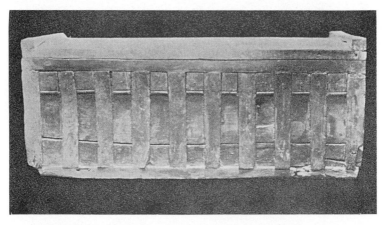

(b) Wooden coffin for an extended burial, Second Dynasty

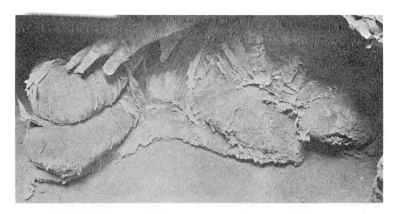

(a) Uncoffined 'mummy' of the Second Dynasty

(b) Coffin in a burial niche of the Second Dynasty

Burial of a dog at the entrance gate of the tomb of Queen Her-nit at Sakkara

Remains of two wooden statues in the funerary temple of Ka'a at Sakkara

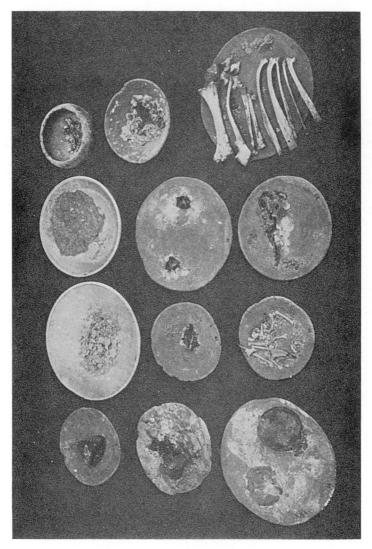

The funerary repast laid out on stone and pottery dishes

Funerary repast as found in an intact tomb of the Second Dynasty at Sakkara

(b) Ivory statuette from
Abydos

(a) The stela of the nobleman Merka
from the tomb of Ka'a at Sakkara

Schist statue of Kha-sekhem from Hieraconpolis

(a) Funerary stela of the Second Dynasty, from Sakkara

(b) Part of a limestone lintel carved with a frieze of lions. From the burial chamber of the tomb of Queen Her-nit at Sakkara

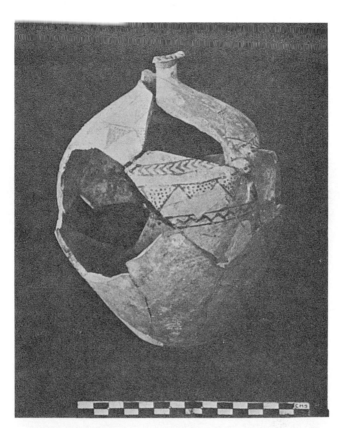

(a) Foreign pottery dated to the late First Dynasty

(b) Small alabaster bowl of floral design. Second Dynasty

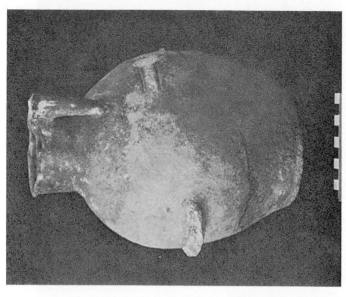

(b) Foreign pottery dated to the middle of the First Dynasty

(a) Foreign pottery dated to the late First Dynasty

(b) Alabaster bowl of the Second Dynasty from Sakkara

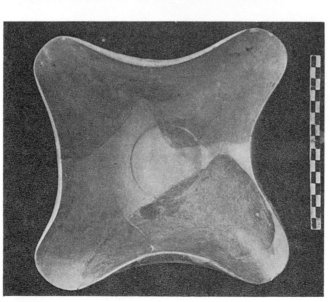

(a) Yellow limestone bowl of the First Dynasty from Sakkara

35

Alabaster vessels from the tomb of Hor-aha at Sakkara

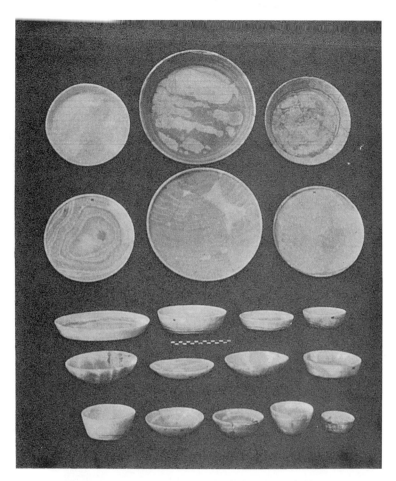

Alabaster vessels from the tomb of Hor-aha at Sakkara

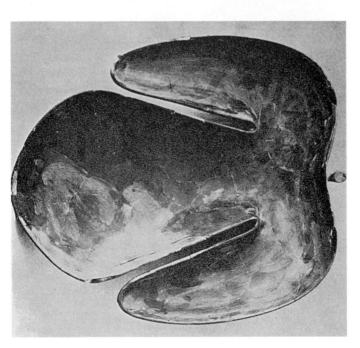

(a) Leaf-shaped dish of schist. Dated to the middle First Dynasty

(b) Cup of schist and pink limestone, from the tomb of Queen Her-nit at Sakkara

38

(b) Dish of schist in the form of a reed basket. Dated to the Second Dynasty

(a) Fragments of a leaf-shaped dish of schist and a spoon of schist. Dated to the middle of the First Dynasty

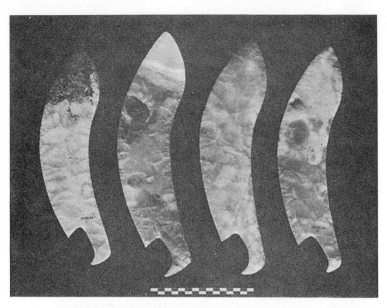

(a) Flint knives dated to the middle First Dynasty

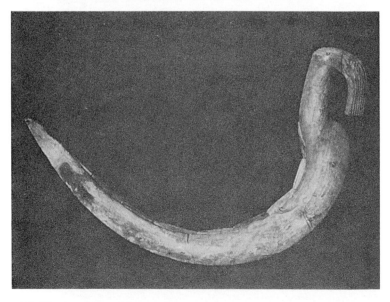

(b) Wooden sickle with inset flint cutting edge. Dated to the middle of
the First Dynasty

Copper tools, weapons, and vessels as found in the tomb of Zer at Sakkara

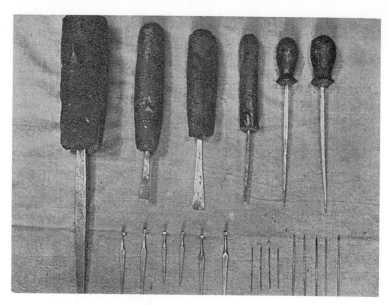

(a) Copper chisels, bodkins, and needles from the tomb of Zer at Sakkara

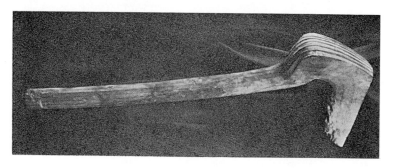

(b) Carved wooden hoe handle. Dated to the First Dynasty

(a) Copper vessels from the tomb of Zer at Sakkara

(b) Copper dishes from the tomb of Zer at Sakkara

(a) Hoes with copper blades and wooden handles. Dated to the middle
First Dynasty

(b) Adzes with copper blades and wooden handles. Dated to the middle
of the First Dynasty

(a) Copper saw and knives. Dated to the middle of the First
Dynasty

(b) Gold plated mace handle from Nubia. Dated to the First Dynasty

45

(b) Gaming disc of black steatite inlaid with alabaster. Dated to the First Dynasty. From Sakkara

(a) Pottery lion of the Second Dynasty. From Hieraconpolis

Circular wooden box inlaid with ebony. Dated to the First Dynasty. When found, it contained a roll of uninscribed papyrus. From Sakkara

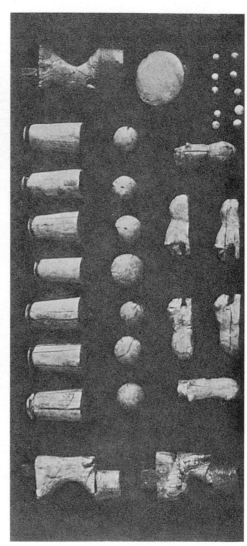

Ivory gaming sets from the tomb of Uadji at Sakkara

48

and weapons. In fact all the objects which made life comfortable were to supply the same service in the after life, as were the servants of the kings who accompanied their master in death. The tomb was designed as his house and, like a house, frequently had gardens attached to it; in some tombs of the Second Dynasty we even find lavatories constructed near the burial chamber, within the substructure of the tomb. In fact, unlike the Christian, the Egyptian believed that 'you could take it with you'; hence the elaborate funerary installation which must have represented a large proportion of his material wealth accumulated during life.

In the following review of typical burials of various classes of society throughout the 450 years of Egypt's Archaic Period, we can observe the developments of the architectural genius of these people; change followed change, reflecting the increasing prosperity which Unification had brought to the land. But not all these changes were for the better; they were dictated by the increasing awareness of the designers of funerary architecture of the dangers of tomb robbery. In order to protect the valuable equipment of the dead, the burial chambers were cut deeper and protected with stone portcullis blockings. Other changes were probably caused by the development of new religious conceptions, but of this we have only the vaguest knowledge until the excavator can give us more material for research. However, in spite of all the changes and development, the fundamental design of the tombs of the archaic Egyptian remained the same throughout the period: a substructure built below ground level, covered by a brick superstructure in the form of an oblong rectangular platform built in imitation of the dwelling house or palace of the period. Archaeologists speak of these superstructures as 'mastabas', adopting the name given to them by Egyptian workmen who saw in a general form their resemblance to the stone or brick-built bench called a *mastaba* in Arabic which is a common feature of the exterior of their homes.

The evolution in architectural design of the tombs may be roughly divided into six developments, which for the sake of convenience we term early, middle, and late of the First Dynasty, and early, middle, and late of the Second Dynasty. It will be understood that these phases of development have no hard and fast lines of demarcation and the designs of the tombs and funerary customs overlapped from one period to another, depending largely on the locality of the burial and the inclinations and social status of the individual. But in general, in the Memphite area, we can trace certain well-defined changes. In the south at Abydos, the superstructures of the royal tombs or cenotaphs were certainly entirely different in design from their counterparts in the north. No trace of them remains, but, from evidence found at Sakkara, it would appear probable that in the early part of the First Dynasty the superstructure consisted of a rectangular tumulus of rubble cased with brick, which later developed into a stepped pyramid structure similar to that found above the tomb of Enezib at Sakkara. However, the substructures of the Abydos monuments in general conform to the same line of evolution as at Sakkara. Again, for the convenience of this review, we may divide the burial installations of each of the six periods into four classes: 1. that of the kings and higher nobility; 2. the lesser nobility and aristocracy; 3. the minor officials and artisans; and 4. the peasantry. In the early First Dynasty, the tombs of the kings and great nobles consisted of a shallow pit, cut not more than four metres below ground level, in which a series of brick-built rooms was erected, the central and largest being reserved for the burial and the rest to accommodate all the more precious objects of the funerary equipment. This substructure was roofed with timber beams and planks and the mouth of the pit above it filled with rubble. Above this substructure, on ground level, was erected the 'mastaba', a rectangular mass of brickwork with an elaborate panelled exterior and its hollow interior divided up into a series of magazines in which was placed the less valuable funerary equipment. These magazines were roofed with heavy timber; the outer walls of the mastabas were raised aloft to a much greater height than the interior walls, leaving a great intervening space which was filled with rubble forming a core of the mass of the superstructure up to a height of not less than 7 metres. The whole of the panelled exterior of the mastaba was painted in gay colours in designs which imitated the matwork which adorned the outside of the dwelling places of the living; for of course the tomb was a copy of the house or palace of the owner in life (Fig. 79). It is very likely that the top of the mastaba was curved with a flat parapet at each end, as shown in the coffins of the late Second Dynasty (Fig. 77). So much for the actual structure of the tomb, which was usually surrounded by an enclosure wall beyond which were sometimes rows of graves of the owner's servants buried with him for his service in the after life. On the north side of the building was a long brick structure which must have looked rather like the hull of an old-fashioned submarine. This structure contained a wooden boat which was to take the spirit of the dead owner on his voyage with the sun-god (Fig. 78).

We have as yet no satisfactory evidence regarding the actual method of interment, for there was no recognized method of entry to the burial chamber. It is possible that the superstructure was not raised until the burial chamber was occupied and the adjoining rooms filled with their contents. In some burials at Sakkara, there are indications that a corridor in the superstructure leading to the centre of its interior was kept open for the passage of the actual burial; but even then the body of the deceased would have to be lowered

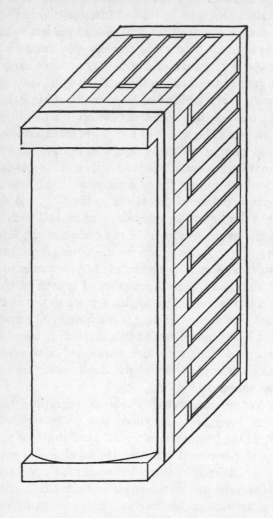

SCALE 0 10 20 30 40 50 60 70 80 90 1 METRE

Fig. 77. Wooden coffin of the late Second Dynasty from Sakkara

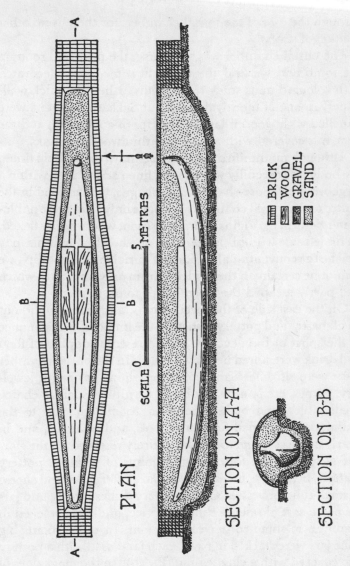

PLAN

SCALE 0 5 METRES

SECTION ON A-A

BRICK
WOOD
GRAVEL
SAND

SECTION ON B-B

Fig. 78. Reconstruction of a boat burial

through the roof of the burial chamber, for there is no other method of access.

The burial chamber was, of course, the principal room in the tomb and we find the walls, in some cases, decorated with coloured mats stuck to the walls rather like thick wall-paper. In one of the royal burials at Sakkara, pilasters were panelled with wood inlaid with strips of gold plate, and the floor was covered with evenly laid thin wooden planks.

Although mummification was not known in archaic times, the body was carefully wrapped in linen and placed within a large wooden house-shaped sarcophagus, which stood in the centre of the burial chamber. We have only found one noble-man's body in its original burial position, where he lay flexed, on his left side with his head to the north. Although this may well be the conventional position of burial for the nobility, we cannot be certain on the evidence from only one tomb which had partly escaped the attention of tomb robbers.

On the east side of the sarcophagus, a repast was laid out on alabaster and pottery dishes for the immediate sustenance of the spirit of the deceased, while reserve supplies of food and drink were stored near by (Pl. 29). In the burial chamber there were also chests and boxes containing garments, jewel-lery, games, etc., and ivory inlaid furniture, such as chairs, small tables, and beds. The other rooms adjacent to the burial also contained furniture, tools, and weapons, and in nearly every case one room was entirely reserved for the stor-age of food in the form of great joints of meat on pottery platters, bread kept in sealed globular pottery jars, and cheese in small tubular vessels. Other pottery dishes, bowls, and jars formed a sort of reserve dinner service, and were stacked in readiness in some corner of the room. In other rooms big wine jars were stacked in rows, each jar closed with a pottery cap covered with a clay sealing (Pl. 20). In the magazines of the superstructure, more equipment was stored, and in the bigger tombs each room seemed to be reserved for special classes of objects, tools and weapons in one, games in another, and above all more stores of food and drink. Such great treasure houses as these could not escape the attention of plunderers for long, but sufficient remains for us to reconstruct with certainty the general set-up of these great tombs, which is shown in Fig. 79.

The tombs of the lesser nobility were similar in general design, although considerably smaller. Unfortunately, all examples of this class of tomb yet found have had their brick superstructures destroyed and there is no evidence to show whether they also had the elaborate panelled exterior of the great tomb; but on balance it is probable that they had. The niches would be built on the same scale, but there would of course be a smaller number, and on such a tomb as No. 1532 of Naga-ed-der (shown, restored, in Fig. 80) there would perhaps be two large niches on the short sides and four on the long. From other evidence, it would appear probable that magazines were not built within the superstructure, for the burial chamber and subsidiary rooms would be sufficient to accommodate the more limited wealth of the lesser nobility. In general the substructures of such tombs follow the general design of a central room for the burial and two rooms on each side of it for funerary equipment, which was similar in general character to that of their superiors, although naturally of poorer quality.

To illustrate the burials of the artisans and servant class who accompanied their masters in death, we have as examples only the tombs which surround the great funerary monuments of the kings and nobility. Those domestics were sacrificed, whether willingly or otherwise we do not know, but there is no reason to suppose that the arrangement of their burial was any different from other members of their class who had died naturally. The tomb consists of a single

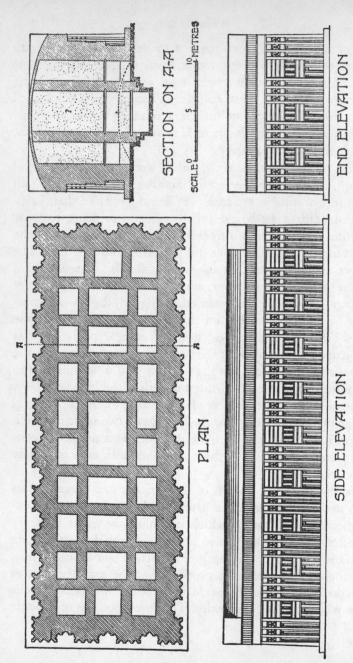

PLAN

SECTION ON A-A

SCALE 0 5 10 METRES

END ELEVATION

SIDE ELEVATION

Fig. 79. Reconstruction of the exterior of a brick superstructure

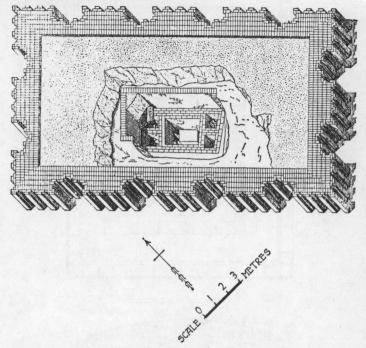

Fig. 80. Reconstruction of Tomb 1532 at Naga-ed-der

oblong pit roofed with timber and covered with a low rectangular superstructure with a rounded top (Fig. 81). The
body was usually contracted on the left side with the head to
the north, but this orientation was not strictly adhered to.
Wrapped in linen, it was placed in a small wooden coffin.
Wine and food jars were invariably placed outside the coffin,
but the character of other objects varied considerably according to the profession and sex of the deceased. The burials
outside the tomb of Queen Meryet-nit at Sakkara showed a
great variety of funerary furniture to suit the services of each
individual occupant: copper and flint tools for the craftsman,
paint pots for the artist, model ships for the sailor, knives and

137

SCALE 0 |_____|_____| METRE

Fig. 81. Tomb of the artisan and servant class of the early First Dynasty

meat for the butcher, toilet utensils for the women. In the south at Abydos, small stone stelae crudely inscribed with the name of the deceased are frequently found with burials of this class, but because of the complete destruction of the superstructure, no indication remains of their original position; presumably they were on the surface, perhaps embedded in the superstructure (Fig. 25). At Sakkara, no such monuments have been discovered, but this may be because of the widespread removal of stone in this area.

The graves of the peasantry differ little from those of the late predynastic type and it is obvious that in the early part of the First Dynasty the mass of the people were unaffected by the funerary customs of their superiors who, as previously pointed out, were probably distinct racially. The graves are generally oval or oblong pits with rounded corners, cut in the gravel and surmounted after burial by a circular low mound made from the filling taken from the grave pit. The contracted body of the owner, nearly always on the right side with the head south, usually lay on a reed mat; but in the more wealthy burials it is sometimes encased by an erection of wooden planks. Pottery and stone vessels with copper and flint tools and toilet implements were placed by the side of the burial. After the interment, the grave was roofed with sticks and matting, above which was a filling of sand and rubble. Fig. 82 shows a typical burial of this character.

By the middle of the First Dynasty, the increase in size and elaboration of the great tombs of the kings and great nobles necessitated an easier means of entry for the burial, and in consequence we have the introduction of the stairway tomb in the reign of Udimu. The transition from the earlier type of tomb is shown in the sumptuous burial dated to Uadji, Udimu's predecessor, which we discovered at Sakkara in 1953 (Fig. 83). Although not a stairway tomb, its vast size and greatly enlarged substructure show the necessity for some

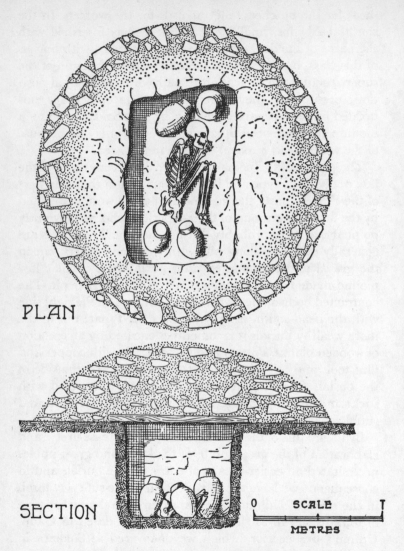

PLAN

SECTION

0   SCALE

METRES

Fig. 82. Tomb of the poorer class of the early First Dynasty

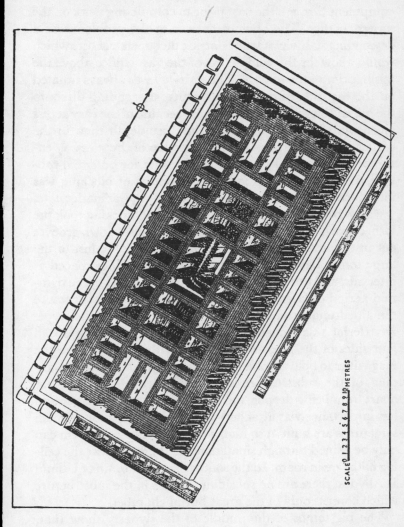

SCALE 0 1 2 3 4 5 6 7 8 9 10 METRES

Fig. 83. Axonometric drawing of Tomb 3504 at Sakkara

method of access other than lowering the body and funerary equipment through the roof prior to completing work on the superstructure. The obvious answer to the problem was a descending stairway starting outside the superstructure which would allow for the completion of the vast edifice above the tomb, prior to the funeral. The stairway was always situated on the east side of the superstructure, descending direct to the burial chamber which perhaps, because of the easy access given by it, was cut to a much greater depth than in the earlier monuments. But the introduction of the stairway entrance also made entry to the tomb easier for potential robbers, and to prevent plundering, a system of blocking was introduced which although, as we now know, was inadequate, was nevertheless ingenious. This system of blocking took the form of great stone slabs lowered as portcullises down grooves cut in the side walls of the stairway (Fig. 84). Most of the large tombs have three stone portcullis blockings spaced at intervals, and this method of protection survived in the pyramid period of later times. The design of the superstructure remained unaltered and, as with tombs of the earlier type, its exterior was embellished with recessed panelling on all four sides of the great oblong mass within which were the magazines to hold surplus funerary equipment. But the planning of the substructure shows considerable change, for apart from being deeper, the burial chamber was larger and less importance was attached to the subsidiary rooms which sometimes are built at so high a level that access to them can only be gained through small doors set high up near the ceiling of the main room. In the southern type of tomb of Udimu at Abydos, there are no subsidiary rooms in the substructure which consists only of the great burial chamber.

The big tombs of the middle of the dynasty show that, apart from the introduction of the stairway, it was a period of considerable architectural change and experiment, and

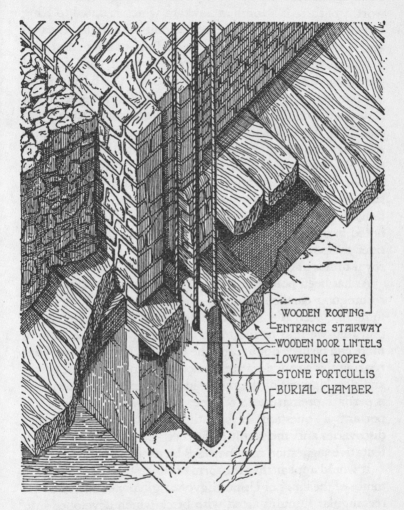

WOODEN ROOFING
ENTRANCE STAIRWAY
WOODEN DOOR LINTELS
LOWERING ROPES
STONE PORTCULLIS
BURIAL CHAMBER

Fig. 84. Detail of portcullis blocking in stairway entrance

each monument shows differences in design. Most note-worthy of these is a tomb at Sakkara which is dated to King Enezib and which may well be his tomb. When first excava-ted, it appeared to be a conventional form of the period with a typical mastaba superstructure decorated with recessed panelling. A descending stairway led down to a burial cham-ber flanked by two subsidiary rooms built at a higher level. But in clearing the interior of the mastaba superstructure in search of the usual magazines, we found a second super-structure concealed within the first. This structure was of entirely different design, being in step pyramid form, as shown in Fig. 45. Although it is only in this tomb that we have found such a structure preserved, traces of the founda-tions of what may have been similar buildings have been noted in other large tombs of the period, and we must con-sider the possibility of its being a common feature of all the royal tombs at Sakkara.

As has been pointed out on p. 84, the original form was a rectangular earthen tumulus with a brick casing, as in the tomb of Queen Her-nit, which developed into the step pyra-mid that we find in the tomb of Enezib. Of this evolution there can be little doubt, and the question then arises of what bearing this strange feature has on the problem of the origin and development of the pyramid structure of later times. It is perhaps premature to put forward a hypothesis on so im-portant a question before the achievement of further discoveries and the result of further research, but at least a tentative suggestion may perhaps be excused.

It would appear that the form of superstructure above the tombs of the kings of Upper Egypt originally consisted of the rectangular tumulus faced with brick which developed into the superstructure of elongated pyramid form. In Lower Egypt, the superstructure above the royal tombs took the form of the mastaba with its panelled façade. At Sakkara, notably in the case of the tombs of Queen Her-nit and Ene-zib, the two forms of superstructure were welded together in one building: the tumulus pyramid directly over the burial, and surrounded and covered by the walls of the palace façade mastaba. Comparison of the plans of the tombs of Her-nit and Enezib with that of the step pyramid enclosure of King Zoser of the Third Dynasty reveals such similarities in design and proportion that we may well consider the design of the latter to be a development of the composite royal tomb of the First Dynasty (Fig. 85).

Our knowledge of the religious thought and symbolism be-hind the architectural designs of the funerary structures of early Egypt is almost non-existent. But on the grounds of pure architectural evolution it is not unreasonable to envisage the gradual reduction of a palace façade mastaba to a recessed enclosure wall which surrounded the greatly enlarged and heightened pyramid structure covering the burial chamber.

It is not possible within the compass of this book to expand this interesting question, but progress in this research is being made, and it is hoped that future excavation, particularly in the tombs of the Second Dynasty, may yield evidence in support or otherwise of what at present can only be offered as a rather nebulous hypothesis.

In the arrangement of the burial and the funerary equip-ment there was no change and the big wooden sarcophagus was surrounded by food and drink and all the owner's most precious possessions. The question of sustenance for the spirit of the owner is perhaps stressed more in the burials of this period than in the earlier ones – vast quantities of meat, bread, and wine were stored in the magazines, and in one tomb we found built-in grain bins, so that the owner could replenish his stock of bread when the need arose. Another example of such forethought was the supply of natural flint nodules buried with flint knives, so that

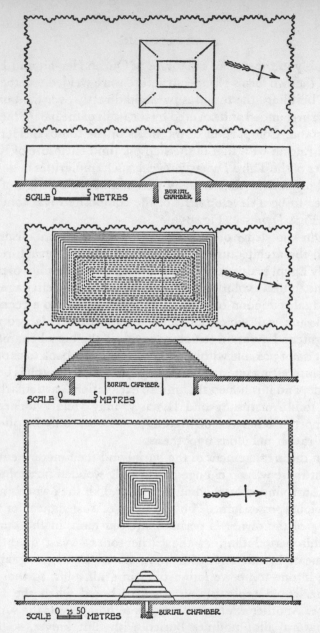

Fig. 85. Sketch-plans of the tombs of Her-nit (early First Dynasty),
Enezib (late First Dynasty), and Zoser (early Third Dynasty)

the deceased could make more of these tools should they be broken.

The tombs of the lesser nobility are just smaller editions of the larger burials, but, as in the earlier parts of the dynasty, the smaller superstructures appear to have had a solid core of rubble or brick, with no magazines within the interior. Examples with a panelled exterior such as No. 1374 at Helwan (Fig. 86) are typical of the period, but a plain façade to the superstructure is also common, particularly in the smaller tombs. The substructure consists of a burial chamber with two or more subsidiary rooms with floors at a higher level, all roofed with timber.

With burials of the artisan class, there appears to be little or no change from those of the earlier part of the dynasty which are described above. The only new development appears to be the introduction of a false door at the south end of the east façade of the superstructure (Fig. 87). The mass of the common people continued to bury their dead in the pit graves of their ancestors, raising above them a circular superstructure of rubble. But graves of the more important among them begin to show a tendency to copy, to adopt some of the structural refinements of their superiors. The use of brick linings to the oblong pits and the placing of the contracted bodies in some primitive form of wooden coffin becomes more common. Fig. 88 shows a typical burial of this type.

In the latter part of the First Dynasty there were considerable changes in the architectural design of tombs of every class, and although some of the greater monuments tend to retain the general plan of earlier times, most of those that can be dated to the close of the period show a fundamental change in conception. With the notable exception of the great tomb dated to King Ka'a at Sakkara (Fig. 53), the recessed panelling on the exterior of the superstructure disappears and the plain face of the exterior walls is relieved

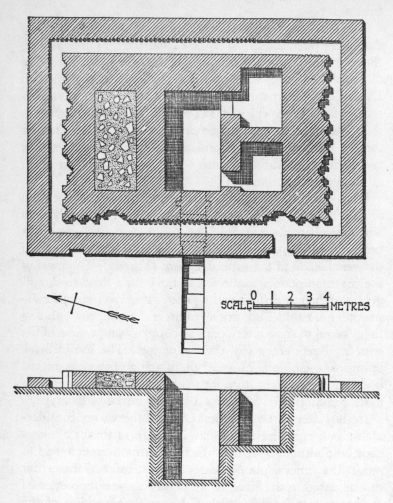

SCALE 0 1 2 3 4 METRES

Fig. 86. Plan of Tomb 1374 at Helwan

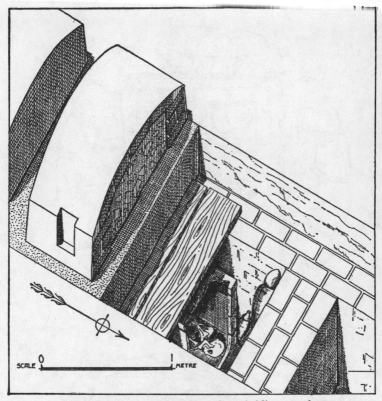

SCALE 0   1 METRE

Fig. 87. Axonometric view of a subsidiary tomb
of the middle First Dynasty

only by two false doors at the south and north ends of the east
façade. Moreover, the superstructure is no longer hollow
with magazines, but has a solid core of rubble or brickwork.
The direct stairway entrance to the substructure gives place
to one of L-shaped plan, which although starting on the east
side of the tomb, enters the burial chamber from the north.
With this innovation the axis of the substructure is changed
from east–west to north–south and the rooms subsidiary to
the burial chamber are no longer immediately adjacent to it,

149

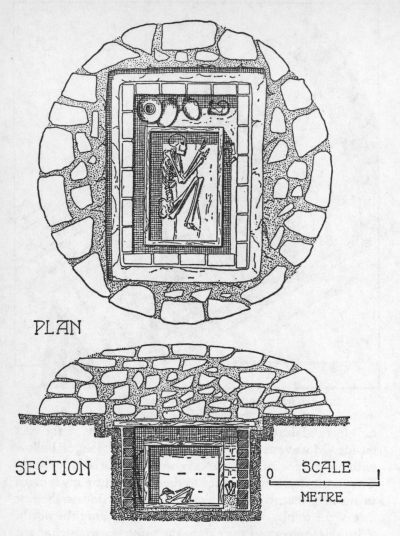

PLAN

SECTION

SCALE

0   METRE

Fig. 88. Poor-class burial of the middle First Dynasty

but are on each side of the entrance stairway with which they
are connected by doorways. The north–south axis of the substructure is usual, but in the larger tombs there are exceptions and in these the old east–west axis is retained with a
direct entrance stairway from the east. But the new plan of
subsidiary rooms opening from the stairway before it reached
the burial chamber has been adopted even where the earlier
rule of the burial axis has been retained. The two great monuments of Ka'a at Abydos and Sakkara show this feature, but
in general the new design (as shown in Fig. 89) of the sub-

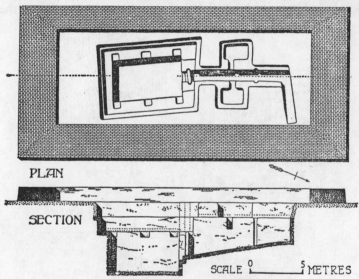

Fig. 89. Plan and section of Tomb 3338 at Sakkara

structure was prevalent at the close of the dynasty and was
the direct forerunner of the Second Dynasty design and ultimately of tomb planning of much later periods, surviving
even in the rock tombs of the New Kingdom more than 1500
years later.

The change in architectural design did not extend to the

method of burial which, as far as can be ascertained, remained the same. However, one fact must be noted: apart from the royal burials, the funerary equipment appears more limited in quantity than in earlier times and this may be a reflection of the extra expenditure forced on the owner by the erection of more elaborate tomb structures. The burial chamber now appears to be sufficient for the storage of all the funerary furniture and the contents of the subsidiary rooms were restricted to food and drink for the spirit of the deceased. The burial of servants and retainers around the burial of the kings and great nobles, although it appears to survive in the

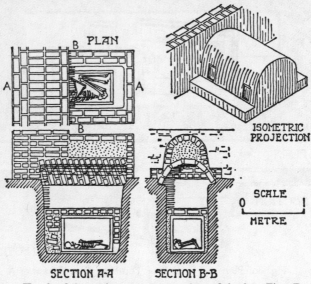

Fig. 90. Tomb of the artisan or servant class of the late First Dynasty

south, has ceased in the north, and although subsidiary tombs have been found within the enclosure of a big tomb of the period, at Sakkara, their arrangement does not suggest that the owners died other than natural deaths.

Recent excavations at Helwan have revealed many tombs

of the lesser nobility which can be dated to the latter part of the dynasty, and these burials conform to the same plan and general arrangements as the bigger structures at Sakkara.

The graves of the artisan class differ little from those of earlier times, except that the superstructure is higher, with two false doors at the north and south ends of the east façade. Here, again, we are dependent for our knowledge of the design of such tombs on subsidiary burials, but we have no reason to doubt that they are fairly representative of the burial installations of this class of society during the period. Fig. 90 shows details of the construction of tombs of this type and the general arrangement of the burial.

The graves of the peasantry show no change in the latter part of the dynasty, except perhaps a further increase in the use of brick linings to the burial pits and the use of coffins in the case of the more wealthy interments.

With the advent of the Second Dynasty, a radical development in the design and construction of funerary structures took place. Even as early as the middle of the First Dynasty there are isolated examples of the burial chamber being excavated in the rock and not formed by an open working with an artificial roof. But this practice was comparatively rare and it was only at the end of the First Dynasty that the system of open working was abandoned in favour of excavation in regard to the subterranean parts of the tomb structure (Fig. 91).

In the earlier half of the Second Dynasty, the tombs of the great nobles followed closely on the design common at the end of the preceding dynasty with the difference that the L-shaped entrance stairway descended to a greater depth and both the magazines on each side of it and the burial chamber itself were excavated and not formed by open workings (Fig. 93). No longer is the entrance passage roofed with timber, but great stone flags were found more practical. In the

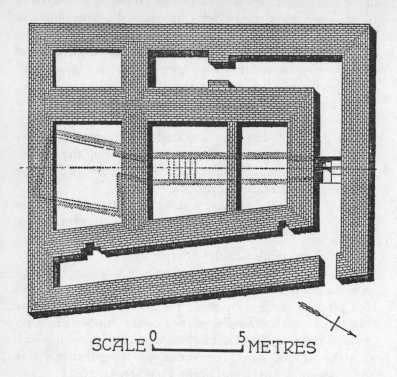

SCALE 0 [——————] 5 METRES

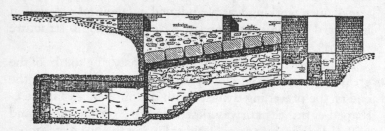

Fig. 91. Rock-cut tomb of the late First Dynasty

rock-cut burial chamber we have the forerunner of the subterranean 'house' of the later part of the dynasty, for it is divided into separate rooms with the burial compartment on the west side. But the construction still followed the pattern of the First Dynasty in dividing the compartment into separate rooms by brick walls instead of cutting the various chambers out of the living rock (Fig. 92). Henceforth the burial com-

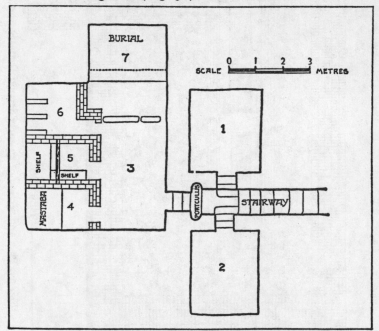

Fig. 92. Substructure of an early Second Dynasty tomb

partment corresponding to the bedroom of the deceased's house in life is always on the west side of the complex of rooms which represented the other parts of his domicile. The wooden coffin was, in these earlier Second Dynasty tombs, placed on a raised platform just as his bed would be so placed in his home in life. It is unfortunate that all such

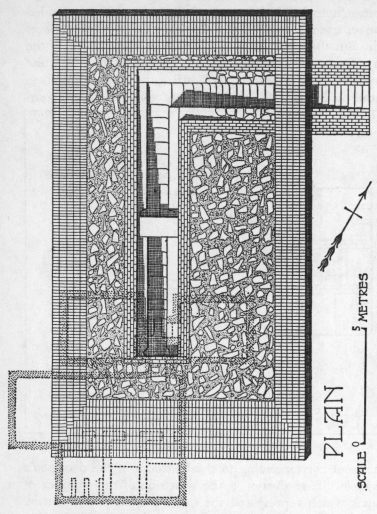

PLAN

SCALE 0 _____ 5 METRES

Fig. 93. Plan and section of an early Second Dynasty tomb

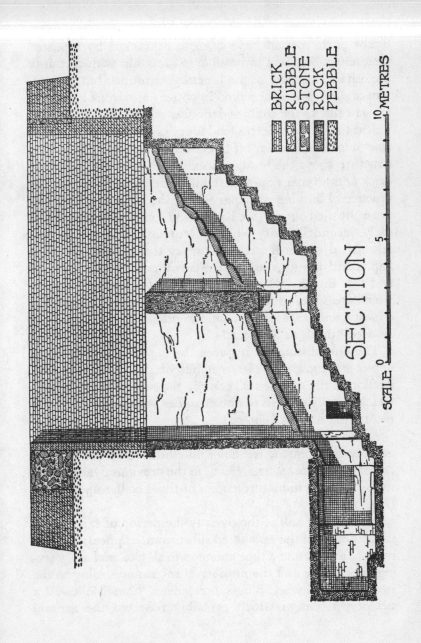

BRICK
RUBBLE
STONE
ROCK
PEBBLE

SECTION

SCALE 0 .... 5 .... 10 METRES

tombs of the period have been so ransacked by repeated plundering that it is impossible to ascertain with certainty the original position of the funerary furniture; but the custom of placing a meal served in pottery and stone vessels on the east side of the coffin is definitely established (Pl. 29), as well as the storage of extra food supplies in the exterior magazine outside the house, off the entrance passage. The superstructure above the tomb was solid with a core of rubble or brick and no magazines were built within it. However, the practice of burying offerings within the superstructure had not quite died out and we have found some big tombs of the early Second Dynasty with large quantities of pottery vessels buried within the rubble core of the superstructure, in haphazard groups, rather like currants in a cake (Pls. 12 and 13). But this was only a survival of a funerary custom which was out of fashion even in the latter part of the previous dynasty, and it was not a common practice, existing only in isolated burials at Sakkara.

The only distinction between the big tombs of the great nobles and those of the lesser nobility is one of size and a reduction in the number of rooms in the subterranean 'house' which usually consists of one chamber with a side compartment for the coffin (Fig. 94).

As the custom of burying retainers round the tombs of the nobility had ceased, we have no evidence of the form of burial of the artisan class, but as in the previous dynasty they were probably miniature copies of those of the upper class (Fig. 95).

In the latter half of the dynasty the period of experiment in the design of the excavated substructure appears to have come to an end and a type common to all had evolved, varying only in size and the number of rooms, according to the wealth of the owner. The subterranean 'house' followed a stereotyped design which probably reflected the general

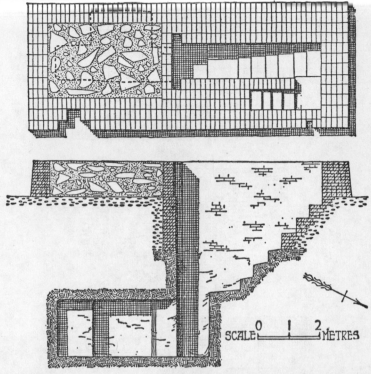

Fig. 94. Plan and section of a Second Dynasty tomb of the middle class

arrangement of dwellings of the period, with its great reception hall on each side of which are bedrooms for guests, etc. (Fig. 96). The innermost part of the 'house' was reserved for the household, consisting of the master's bedroom (burial chamber) opening from the west side of a living-room, on the other side of which is the harem quarter. Both the harem and the master's quarters have a double access to a bathroom and lavatory. The magazines opening from the stairway entrance represent the store-rooms outside the house, and naturally it is in these that food, wine, and surplus funerary furniture was placed.

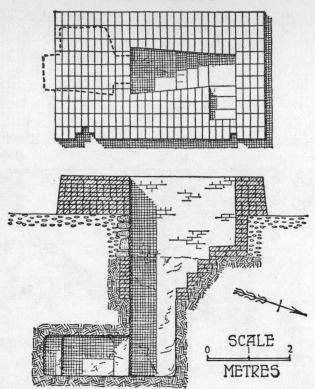

Fig. 95. Plan and section of a Second Dynasty tomb of the poorer class

The system of blocking the stairway entrance with stone portcullises continued and the number of such safeguards varies between one and three according to the size of the tomb.

The brick superstructure was solid with a filling of rubble, and the exterior walls were plain with two false doors, the larger at the south end and the smaller at the north end of the east façade. It would appear that the rubble core of the superstructure was deposited after the burial, for, unlike the First Dynasty practice, the head of the entrance stairway was not outside the superstructure but was buried below it.

The only two funerary structures of the Second Dynasty that can definitely be assigned to royalty are those of Perabsen and Kha-sekhemui at Abydos (Figs. 60 and 66). Both these tombs are entirely different in design from those of the same period in the north, which is strange, for although the superstructures of the southern tombs must have been different, the substructures at Abydos follow the same general lines of development as the funerary structures in the north. Both monuments follow the general design of a free-standing burial chamber surrounded by rows of magazines all

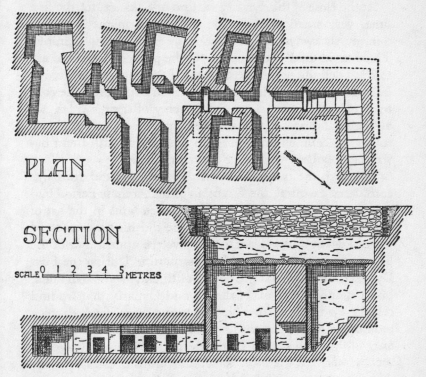

PLAN

SECTION

SCALE 0 1 2 3 4 5 METRES

Fig. 96. Plan and section of the substructure of a
late Second Dynasty tomb

constructed in an open-worked pit. The difference in architectural conception is so radical, however, that one is tempted to see in these strange buildings some connexion with the adoption of Set worship by Perabsen and its apparent toleration under Kha-sekhemui.

The tombs of the lesser nobility follow the same design but with very few exceptions there are no magazines on each side of the entrance stairway and the 'house' usually has only a hall and two rooms, one of which, on the west, is the burial chamber.

At the close of the dynasty we find at Sakkara, for the first time, very small shaft tombs with what might be called dummy stairways, of which Fig. 97 is a typical example. These small tombs must belong to the poorer classes and are the first definite sign that the mass of the population were at last adopting the burial customs of their superiors. The contents of such tombs show the poverty of their owners, for although the bodies are wrapped in coarse linen, they are usually uncoffined and carry no possessions with them beyond two pottery vessels for food and drink.

Although the preservation of the bodies of the dead was considered essential, the Egyptian of the Archaic Period had not discovered the methods of his descendants in the art of true mummification. Nevertheless he did his best to retard natural decay and at least to preserve the appearance of the living person on the actual bony structure. During the First Dynasty, we know that the body was thickly swathed in linen, but it is only in burials of the Second Dynasty that we find certain evidence of the first tentative steps towards true mummification. This consisted of reproducing the appearance of the dead person by moulding the linen bandages in such a way that the face, torso, and limbs preserve the life shape after the actual body has decayed and shrunk over the skeleton. This was apparently achieved by soaking the linen

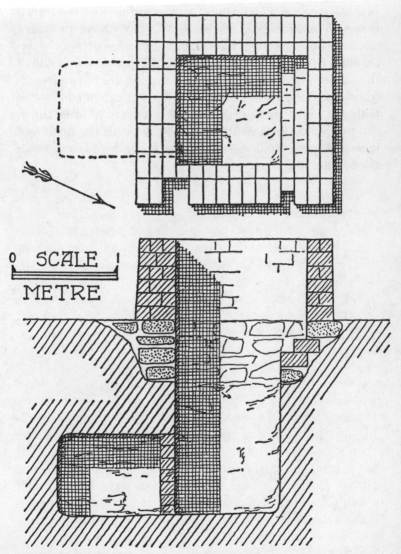

0 SCALE
METRE

Fig. 97. Plan and section of a poor-class tomb of the late Second Dynasty

in some gummy material and so successful were the results that such 'mummies' of the Second Dynasty have an almost uncanny appearance of life (Pl. 25a). The features of the deceased are modelled in detail, as are the genital parts, and in the case of women the breasts and nipples are shown in perfect form. Such bodies are not laid in an extended position with the limbs concealed, like the mummy of later times, but are placed in a contracted posture with the arms and legs, and even the fingers, separated, bandaged, and modelled in life-like form.

Chapter 5

ART

As in architecture, sculpture, painting, and decorative design underwent a radical change with the advent of the dynastic race. A new art came to Egypt, and although many authorities see in it an unbroken development from that of the predynastic age, as exemplified in the white-line drawings on pottery, I think there is overwhelming evidence of the incursion into the Nile valley, in the period immediately prior to the Unification, of something entirely new.

SCULPTURE IN RELIEF

For the first time we see an art which is the undoubted forerunner of that of Pharaonic Egypt – conceptions in sculpture and decorative design which were to endure for more than 3000 years. Connecting links with the art of the Predynastic period undoubtedly existed and in its new environment it is not surprising that the artist adopted certain characteristics from the work of his predecessors; but in all essentials it was the product of a new civilization. This new art undoubtedly owed much to Mesopotamian influence, the evidence of which has been listed by the late Dr Henri Frankfort as follows: 1. Composite animals, especially winged griffins and serpent-necked felines, on palettes and knife-handles; 2. Group of hero dominating two lions; 3. Pairs of entwined animals on knife-handles and the Narmer palette. But this Mesopotamian influence, direct or indirect, was only transitory; after the Unification it disappeared and the pure conventions of

Egyptian art became established. Our knowledge of sculpture in relief for the period preceding the Unification is confined almost entirely to the votive ceremonial stone palettes and mace-heads, most of which were discovered at Hieraconpolis. Both the design and technique of these objects vary considerably, from the crudest products to such finished masterpieces as those described below. But even with this variation in quality, it is apparent that behind them there must have been a considerable period of development, satisfactory evidence of which has not yet been found in Egypt.

Outstanding among the votive palettes is the famous object which records Narmer's conquests. The designs on both sides are well planned, so that the sense of balance, so important in later Egyptian art, is achieved (Fig. 4). We see all the conventional postures of the human and animal figures, so stereotyped in later times, already adopted with confidence by the artist. However, valuable as the Narmer palette is as an example of historical record and of artistic achievement, its fame rests largely on the fact that by fortunate chance it is one of the few important votive objects which has been found unbroken and complete. Other palettes existed which were far superior to it, but unfortunately only fragments of these have as yet been found. For example, the Louvre fragment (Pl. 3b) must have come from a palette far superior to that of Narmer in artistic achievement. The figure of the bull trampling on his prostrate enemy is indeed a masterpiece unexcelled in any other example of archaic Egyptian art. The pressure of the animal's hoof on the calf of the right leg of the human figure is superbly executed, as is the treatment of the upraised hand of the fallen man. Apart from this technical perfection, the design is in itself admirable, particularly when we realize that the upper part of the bull forms the outline of the top of the palette and was probably duplicated in reverse on the left side of the object.

Another outstanding example of decorative design and superb technique are the fragments of a palette, one part of which is in the British Museum and another in the Ashmolean at Oxford. On the obverse is a battle scene with the bodies of the dead being attacked by a lion and by vultures. Above them, captives are held by standards of Horus and Thoth, and opposite them is another defeated enemy held apparently by a man in a long fringed garment which we associate with Mesopotamian fashion. On the reverse are two giraffes feeding from the leaves of a palm tree which divides them.*

The so-called Hunter's palette, parts of which are in the British Museum and the Louvre, is unique in its presentation of massed human figures and the life-like postures of some of them, particularly the running men, one of whom has lassoed a gazelle, while the other seeks to avoid the attention of a wounded lion (Pl. 1b). The hunted animals, consisting of lion, gazelle, deer, fox, rabbit, and ostrich (?), form the axis of the palette and are flanked by the rows of hunters. At the top of the palette is a shrine by the side of which is a double bull.

The serpent-necked felines representative of Mesopotamian art are shown on another palette which is in the Ashmolean at Oxford. Amid the confused mass of natural life we note also such mythological creatures as the winged griffin, a lion with a snake neck, and an upright two-legged figure with a head reminiscent of the mysterious Set animal. Again in this palette the perfect balance and space filling is predominant. The work on all these palettes, which are made of schist, has been executed with a copper scraper or graving tool.

The treatment of animal and human figures on the palettes is repeated on other objects, such as the ivory handles

* Petrie, *Ceremonial Slate Palettes*, Pls. D and E.

of flint knives, like the unique specimens found at Gebel-el-Arak (Fig. 1 and Pl. 1a), and on the embossed gold plate mace-shaft found in northern Nubia (Fig. 72).

In the design on the big votive mace-heads, the symmetry of later times is lacking and indeed the 'space filling' is often gravely at fault; but the use of registers, each representing individual groups, had already been adopted as a method of depiction at an early stage, as in the posture of the human and animal. The finest examples of such objects are the mace-heads of the Scorpion King and Narmer, both of which were found at Hieraconpolis and are now in the Ashmolean at Oxford (Figs. 3 and 5).

The first examples we have of sculpture in relief on a large scale are the royal stelae from Abydos and these show an astonishing variation both in design and technique, unexplainable even when we know that artistic expression on monuments of these dimensions was in its early and experimental stage. The outstanding masterpiece is the stela of King Uadji, a monument which in its beautiful simplicity was never excelled, even in the more sophisticated conceptions of later periods (Pl. 2b). This was indeed the work of a genius and although the other royal stelae are of similar design, they fall far short of it in every way. Some are crudely primitive, both in design and execution, such as those of Queen Meryet-nit, and others like that of King Ka'a, although technically satisfactory, fail in their balance of design, which is usually far too heavy.

Only two private stelae of the First Dynasty can claim any degree of real artistic achievement and they may well be the work of the same sculptor. The stela of the nobleman Sabef was found in the tomb of Ka'a at Abydos and the stela of Merka was found in a great tomb at Sakkara which is probably the northern burial place of the same king. Thus both monuments are of the same date and although found so far apart their workmanship and general design suggest that they may well have had a common origin. The compositions, although crudely executed, are fully developed with the standing and seated figures of their owners facing right and with an array of their titles arranged in horizontal lines. Both stelae appear to be unfinished and evidence of the technique employed is therefore apparent. The stone was rubbed down to a flat smooth surface and on this the design was drawn in black pigment, after which the background was cut back by pounding, so that the figures and hieroglyphs stand out as a smooth surface against a pitted ground. It is almost certain that the rough background would have been smoothed down by the use of a copper chisel and grinding stone and perhaps the edges of the figures would have been bevelled; but owing to the unfinished state of both monuments, we cannot be certain on this point. The frieze of lions on the stone lintel in the tomb of Queen Her-nit, although of crude execution, is of interest, for it is the oldest example of constructional sculpture yet found in Egypt. It can be dated with certainty to the middle of the First Dynasty (Pl. 32b). By the end of the Second Dynasty, monumental reliefs had lost their archaic appearance and the inscribed granite door jambs of Kha-sekhemui, although rather crudely executed, show all the symmetry of the work of the Pyramid Age.

Another delightful artistic product is the yellow limestone stela from Sakkara shown on Plate 32a. The interesting series of stelae found by Zaki Saad at Helwan, although rather crude in workmanship, also shows that the conventional design of later times was already established in the Second Dynasty.

Of relief sculpture on small objects, the outstanding masterpiece is the black steatite disk which was found with many others in Tomb 3035 at Sakkara. These disks may have formed part of a game and although many of them were decorated with inlay and relief work, none can compare with the example shown on Plate 46b. The design depicts a hunting scene with two dogs, one chasing a gazelle and the other throwing a gazelle which it holds by the throat. The black dog is carved in a piece with the body of the disk, with the exception of its white underbelly which is inlaid with alabaster. The black horns and hoofs of the gazelles are also part of the body of the disk, but the rest of the figures of the gazelles and the second dog are inlaid in pink and brown alabaster.

SCULPTURE IN THE ROUND

With the beginning of the Dynastic period, we begin to trace the development of sculpture in the round, not only in the production of small figurines but in statuary of large scale in both stone and wood. Unfortunately, monuments of large size suffer from the destructive hands of vandals, for, unlike small objects of art, they are rarely concealed. Consequently little remains to enable us to form any really sound appreciation of archaic Egypt's achievements in art of this character. However, enough has been recovered to prove to us that such monuments existed, and, in some cases at least, the standard was high.

The earliest examples of large statuary that we have are three crude figures of Min found by Petrie at Coptos. Standing about 13 feet high, these headless statues show the god standing in his characteristic posture, and there can be little doubt of their identity, which is confirmed by incised drawings of Min emblems among other figures on the trunk. But these colossi are primitive indeed and it is questionable whether they truly belong to the new art of the dynastic people, for they stand entirely alone and bear more resemblance to the figurines of the Predynastic age.

Of life-size, or near life-size, statues we have the remains of four, dated to Zer, Udimu, and Ka'a of the First Dynasty. All are of wood and although only fragments, they indicate that the conventional forms of subsequent periods were already in existence. The fragment dated to Zer found at Abydos is part of the breast of a female statuette with necklaces painted on it in red and black. The Udimu fragment appears to be part of a wig from a life-size figure – this also was found at Abydos. The other two fragments consist of the feet, ankles, and calves with rectangular pedestals of two near life-size statues found *in situ* in the mortuary temple of the tomb of Ka'a at Sakkara. The statues, probably male, are standing with the left foot advanced.

Stone statuary of smaller than life size is best represented by five statuettes, one in Berlin, one in New York, and the others in Cairo and Oxford. The Berlin specimen is a seated figure of limestone and probably is to be dated to the beginning of the Second Dynasty. The specimen in New York came from Abydos and is generally considered to be of Second Dynasty date. It represents the seated figure of a woman wearing a long simple robe and a heavy wig, with her hands resting palm downwards on her knees; again a posture common in later times. In Cairo, we have the kneeling figure of an official and this statue can be definitely dated to the middle of the Second Dynasty, because it has inscribed on its shoulder the names of the first three kings of the period. Carved in granite, it shows that even the most refractory materials could be mastered by these early sculptors. Cairo also contains in the Michailides Collection, an interesting statuette of Neteren of the early Second Dynasty. Made of alabaster, 13.5 cm. high, it represents the king wearing the Sed-festival dress and the White Crown, seated on a throne.

But the finest examples of archaic sculpture are the two seated statues of Kha-sekhem, one in schist and the other in limestone. Both were found at Hieraconpolis and one is in

Cairo and the other in Oxford. These statues show a complete mastery of sculpture and depict the king wearing the crown of Upper Egypt and the winding robe of the Sed festival. Around the base of each statue is a row of the contorted bodies of slaughtered enemies, with the inscription 'Northern enemies, 47,209'.

Large-sized animal sculpture was fairly common: seated lions, an ape, and a hippopotamus were all subjects of the craftsmen in hard stone. But such subjects as have been recovered from Coptos, Hieraconpolis, and Abydos are disappointing and do not compare with the pleasing animal portraiture which we find in small carved ivory gaming pieces found in the tomb of Nithotep at Nagadeh. The artists of the period were indeed masters in ivory carving and many of the small figurines of this material, from Hierakonpolis and Abydos, are superb. Outstanding among them is the figure of an aged king wearing the crown of Upper Egypt and wrapped in an embroidered Heb-Sed robe. This small masterpiece has not been identified with any particular monarch, but it is generally considered to belong to the early First Dynasty (Pl. 30b).

PAINTING

The purely decorative art of the Archaic Period may be divided into the painted mural and the carved design on bone, ivory, and wooden objects, principally furniture. It is significant that the main motif of the painted design on the walls of buildings is the pattern derived from woven reed matting; in the carved furniture-fittings, patterns based on the conception of bundles of bound reeds are most common. This is best shown by the designs depicted in Figs. 98 and 99, which are fully representative of such art during the First and Second Dynasties; while the bound-reed design employed in ivory and wood carving becomes comparatively rare in later

BLACK
BLUE
RED
YELLOW
WHITE

Fig. 98. Examples of painted mural decoration

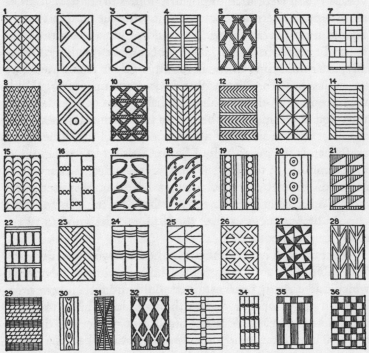

Fig. 99. Examples of decorative design on wood, bone, and ivory

times, nearly all of the multi-coloured patterns of the murals survive throughout Egypt's long history, even in the order of their colour work.

Examples of free-hand brushwork are uncommon, but exist; the most remarkable of them is a roughly shaped rectangular plaque of limestone, found at Sakkara, on which is depicted the figure of a bull and a monkey.

DECORATIVE DESIGN

There were other artists besides the sculptor and the painter; for example, the craftsmen who made the beautiful stone vessels which were such important domestic chattels in archaic Egypt. Sometimes, not content with the simple though beautiful utilitarian forms, he would produce elaborate and fantastic creations which, if they occasionally fail aesthetically, are astonishing in the ingenuity of their technique. The examples shown on Plates 38 and 39 are not unpleasing. With the exception of the leaf-shaped dish which can be dated to the reign of Udimu, they belong to the Second Dynasty. But the most extraordinary of all the creations of the stone vessel craftsmen is the great dish of Sabu. This schist vessel, dated to the middle of the First Dynasty, is apparently carved in imitation of a metal form which had three evenly-spaced parts of the sides bent over towards a hole in the centre. This curious device suggests that the dish was designed to fit on some form of pedestal.

What has survived of the art of the first two dynasties provides abundant testimony to the high level of achievement which had already been attained. Bold and forceful carving, ingenuity of composition, and the technical ability to make use of hard materials foreshadowed that mastery of the arts for which in Pharaonic times the Egyptians became justly famous throughout Western Asia.

Chapter 6

ARCHITECTURE

OUR knowledge of the architecture of archaic Egypt is based almost entirely on funerary monuments, but fortunately these houses of the dead were to a large extent dummy copies of the houses of the living and consequently some conception of domestic buildings is not entirely lacking.

DESIGN

We have reviewed funerary architecture and its development through the First and Second Dynasties in Chapter 4; let us now examine it in relation to the pictorial evidence of temples and other buildings which have been left to us by the contemporary artist. This evidence is rather unsatisfactory, for it is limited to minute drawings on small wooden and ivory labels which, from their unimportant character, did not merit any meticulous accuracy on the part of the draughtsman. Certain shrines are depicted on seal impressions, but here again the picture is so small that the exact character of the structure can only be guessed. There is a tendency among some authorities to consider that the temples and shrines depicted on the labels and seals were flimsy structures of wattle-and-daub. In this identification they are no doubt influenced by the criss-cross lines employed in the drawing, overlooking the fact that this is only a method of hatching common to all such engraved work at this period. It is true that throughout Egyptian history the houses of the living were made of less stable materials than those they employed in the building of the tombs, but I doubt if this would apply to the temples and palaces which I think would be built of the same durable material as the tombs. It is true that all archaic Egyptian architectural forms in brick copied the prototype of wooden structures, but by the time of the foundation of the First Dynasty a fully developed and elaborate brick architecture was flourishing and it is almost certain that the habitual use of the wooden temple and palace had passed, surviving only perhaps in the houses of less important citizens. Once the architects had mastered the problem of building in brick, the mass production of the material would be far more simple than the procuring timber for large buildings in a sparsely wooded land such as Egypt. Indeed we know that all the big timber used in the roofing of the substructures of the big tombs was imported.

The conformity between the temple buildings depicted on the labels and the great panelled brick funerary structures may be demonstrated as deriving from the same architectural conception; fundamentally this was a rectangular building, oblong in plan with a low barrel-vaulted roof with straight end walls, similar in many respects to the wooden coffin shown in Fig. 77. Although such a building has a series of doors on all four sides, the principal entrance appears to have been in the shorter walls at each end. Lighting was obtained from small windows above the doors. The form of this building probably originated in Lower Egypt and it was reproduced in the design of the superstructure of northern tombs throughout the Archaic Period; and in the design of coffins and sarcophagi it survived until the advent of Christianity. Although, as pointed out above, it is probable that these buildings, during the period of the first two dynasties, were built of brick, their general appearance gives an impression that in origin they were frame structures with tented roofing and walls. This impression is heightened by the conventional painted decorations on their panelled walls, which take the form of coloured matting held in place by binding ropes, and of wooden posts which would support the frames on which such matting would hang. But at the period with which we are concerned brick was the medium in which such buildings were constructed, and the intricacies of the elaborate recessed panelling which embellished their exterior cannot be satisfactorily explained as a direct survival of tent framework. All we know is that, with the advent of the dynastic race, this form of monumental architecture makes its first appearance, and it is in this form of building that the Mesopotamian connexion is most apparent. The striking similarities of the recessed brick buildings of both areas is too obvious to be ignored, particularly when we consider that in Egypt there is apparently no background or evidence of development for these immense and intricate structures. But there are also differences, for although the Egyptian architects achieved buildings almost identical in exterior design they reached this result with the employment of a brick of entirely different proportions.* The impression we get is of an indirect connexion, and perhaps the existence of a third party whose influence spread to both the Euphrates and the Nile. But at the present state of our knowledge it is perhaps idle to speculate, and beyond the recognition of the undoubted existence of this connexion, direct or indirect, we cannot go.

It was the square-cut end of buildings of this type that was adopted as the design of the *serech* enclosure in which the

---

* Brick sizes of the Jemdet Nasr period of Mesopotamia:
  20 × 8.50 × 8 cm.
  23 × 9.00 × 6.50 cm.
Brick sizes of the First Dynasty in Egypt:
  24 × 10 × 5 cm.
  23 × 12 × 7 cm.

name of the king was written, known as the Horus name (see Chapter 2). The *serech* enclosure represented the panelled façade of the royal palace, which would be a building similar in outward appearance to the superstructures of the royal tombs. The finest example that we have of the *serech* design is on the famous funerary stela of King Uadji, on which the panelling portrayed on the lower half of the enclosure is exactly reproduced on the brickwork of the big tombs at Sakkara (Fig. 100).

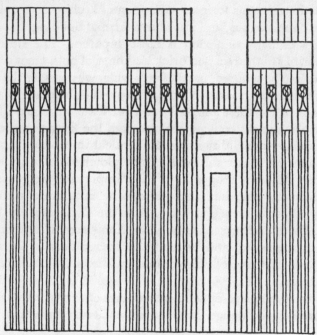

Fig. 100. Palace façade on the stela of Uadji

The early representation of the *serech* palace design on the Narmer palette, for example, shows that such buildings were in existence prior to the actual foundation of united Egypt, and it is important to note that such a design was adopted by the Thinite kings, a fact which brings into question the theory that this architecture belongs entirely to Lower Egypt.

Other architectural forms existed, as we see from the model buildings which were part of the funerary installation of Hor-aha at Sakkara (Fig. 101) and undoubtedly the superstruc-

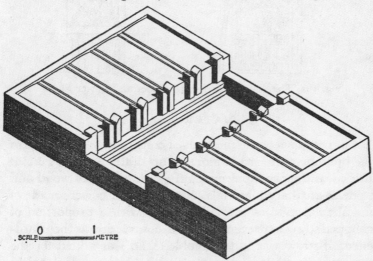

Fig. 101. Isometric view of model building

tures above the royal tombs at Abydos were of radically different design, almost certainly taking the form of a rect-angular brick-cased tumulus which towards the end of the First Dynasty developed into a low stepped pyramid struc-ture like that above Tomb 3504 at Sakkara (Fig. 34).

Wooden building probably survived in the shrines, such as the one which is shown on the label of Udimu from Aby-dos (Fig. 36). This architectural form survived in the design of the innermost shrine in which the figure of the god was housed in the temple sanctuaries of subsequent periods. The two traditional architectural forms shown on Fig. 102 sur-vived as hieroglyphs and were in later times recognized as the ancient national shrines of Lower and Upper Egypt respectively; but whether this was so during the Archaic Period is uncertain.

Fig. 102. The national shrines of Upper and Lower Egypt

MATERIALS

Let us now review the methods of construction employed in the building of the great monuments of the Archaic Period. Brick was the principal medium employed, with wood and stone as auxiliary materials. Sun-dried bricks were made of the alluvial mud of the Nile, mixed with a proportion of chopped straw to prevent excessive contraction as they hardened. If straw was not available, sand was added for the same purpose; but in the period with which we deal, bricks without straw are rare, although the quality of the mud varies considerably even in the same locality and their colour ranges from dark grey to light yellow.

Burnt brick was of course not used in Egypt until Roman times, but it is interesting to note that owing to the destruction by fire of many big tombs of the First Dynasty, the knowledge of burnt brick must have been known to these early builders. Many of the superstructures of the big tombs at Sakkara were turned into brick kilns by the incendiaries and masses of perfect red bricks were exposed to view after their sacrilege. We have evidence that in the restoration of some of these ravaged tombs, original bricks burnt red were re-used by the restorers. Nevertheless, the Egyptian architect was satisfied with his sun-dried brick, and in this he was right, for even today, after 5000 years, these bricks show a hardness almost equal to a soft stone.

Bricks of the Archaic Period vary in size from 23 × 12 × 7 cm. to 26 × 13 × 9 cm., the larger sizes being more favoured during the latter part of the Second Dynasty. Specially small bricks were sometimes employed in the construction of the delicate recessed panelling of the First Dynasty monuments; these were always of a uniform measurement of 17 × 5 × 5 cm. It is important to note that miniature bricks measuring 13.5 × 4.5 × 4.5 cm. were found in the podium or altar of the Eye-Temple at Brak in North Syria. These are dated a little before 3000 B.C.* Sun-dried alluvial mud was also used in the construction of mouldings such as vertical reeding above the panelled façade, the rollers at the top of the smaller niches of panelling and square-cut lintels which were perhaps used in the window panels above the niches (Fig. 103). The quality

Fig. 103. Reconstruction of an early First Dynasty palace façade

*Iraq, IX, Pt I, p. 55, Jemdet Nasr period.

of this material is of extraordinary strength and weight, obtained apparently by reinforcing the mud with small strips of flax linen and drying it when under great pressure. How this pressure was applied we have, as yet, no evidence; but some idea of the hardness and strength of this material can be obtained when we consider a lintel found at Sakkara measuring in its broken state 63 × 18 × 10 cm. – extraordinary dimensions for an object made of sun-dried alluvium.

Stone was not widely used at this period, but there is ample evidence to show that the architects were well aware of its value as a building material and were also capable of working it on a large scale. We find stone employed in retaining walls, beam fillings, flooring, roofing, wall lining, portcullis blocking, and gateways (Pls. 16 and 17). The most commonly used stone was limestone, but granite was also appreciated and roughly dressed blocks of this stone were used as flooring in the tomb of Udimu at Abydos.

Wood in considerable quantities was used in roofing, flooring, and in the facing of wall surfaces of rooms. Egypt was always sparsely wooded, and although local wood may have been used in room linings, etc., the great joists and planking for roofing were imported from Lebanon. Although a certain amount of palm timber must have been available, cedar was the only wood suitable for the span necessary in the large subterranean rooms of the royal tombs.

BUILDING CONSTRUCTION

In wall construction, various bondings of brickwork were used, differing very much according to the width of the wall. The various brick bonds are shown in Figures 104 and 105. In the building of very large walls, at intervals varying between five and eight courses, layers of reed matting were laid to help bind the construction and to dry the interior by

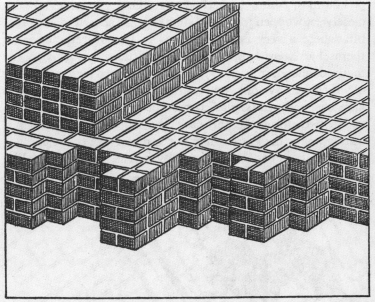

Fig. 104. Examples of brick bonding

conduction. Sometimes, instead of reed mats, a grid of thin sticks was laid on every fifth course. The principle of the buttress to strengthen a wall was known, but was only used on the inner side of walls.

As stated above, stone was often used in retaining walls or revetments, but as such constructions were almost always of a temporary nature, or at least likely to be embedded within the completed building and not seen, only rough-cut blocks were used, held in place with mud mortar. Carefully dressed stone blocks were used in the interior lining of the burial chamber of the tomb of Kha-sekhemui at Abydos, and in the tombs of lesser nobility at Helwan we find the walls of subterranean rooms formed by big slabs of well-dressed limestone. Some of these stone slabs are more than 2 metres in length, 2 metres in height, and .4 metres in thickness.

The most common method of roofing was achieved with closely set wooden joists and planking, as shown in Fig. 106, but where a very large area was to be covered, the joists themselves were supported by longitudinal beams in the methods shown in Fig. 107. Another curious form of roofing of which we have only one example from a big tomb at Sakkara can perhaps be classed more as a ceiling and floor between two stories. In this case, the wooden planks form a ceiling below the joists which are so closely set that the space between them can be spanned by bricks, as shown in Fig.

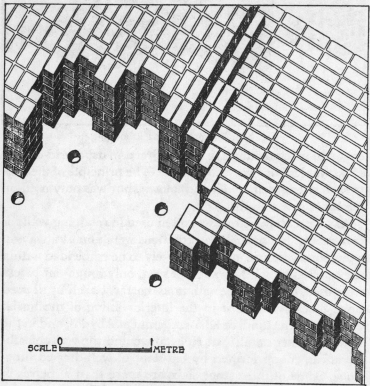

SCALE 0   1 METRE

Fig. 105. Detail of brick construction

184

Fig. 106. Detail of timber roofing

108. Narrow spaces such as corridors or stairways were sometimes roofed with timber beams set together and it was this form of roofing which became conventionalized in stone building in the Pyramid Age (Fig. 109). Small rooms and corridors were also roofed with stone flags, often of a weight out of all proportion to the area they covered.

The leaning barrel vault of brick was known at least as early as the end of the First Dynasty (Fig. 90). Although the examples discovered cover only small grave pits, it would appear from the rounded roofs of model buildings and tops of wooden coffins, which we know were copies of contemporary domestic architecture, that brick vaulting on a larger scale was not impossible to these early builders.

Various methods of flooring were in common use, but the most common was the laying of a level surface of packed alluvium which, after hardening, was covered with a thick gypsum plaster and then left white or painted in other

185

colours. Paving in stone has been found both at Abydos and
Sakkara, but it was not common and was obviously reserved
for important buildings such as the burial chamber of Udimu
at Abydos and one of the rooms of the mortuary temple of a
tomb attributed to Ka'a at Sakkara (Pl. 14). At Abydos the
pavement is of roughly dressed granite slabs, and at Sakkara
it is of hard limestone rectangular slabs of about 90 × 8 cm.
in size, very carefully fitted together on an earthen bed.

Fig. 107. Detail of timber roofing

Fig. 108. Detail of timber roofing

Many of the burial chambers of the royal tombs both in the North and South have wooden plank floors with joist supports below them and shallow skirting board. Details of this method of flooring are shown on Plate 21.

Stairways go back at least to the middle of the First Dynasty, but these early examples, whether built of brick or stone or cut in the living rock, all retain the character of their prototype, the ramp. The riser is vertical but shallow and the 'run' or tread has a fairly steep angle of slope. Towards the end of the Second Dynasty the tread of the stairs tends to get more level, but the slope is never entirely discarded. It is exceptional that the stepped terraces of the inner superstructure of No. 3038 (p. 82) have perfectly vertical riser and horizontal tread. No free-standing stairway of archaic times has yet been found.

Although no actual doors have been preserved, their pivot holes have been found in wooden steps, and it is obvious that

Fig. 109. Detail of timber roofing

the entrance and exit to rooms were protected in this conventional manner. In other words, a barrier which swung on pivots had already been invented in the First Dynasty and probably was in all essentials the same as the wooden doors of the pyramid age which have been preserved, consisting of one or two planks strengthened with horizontal battens.

Again, although no actual window frames have been found, there is certain evidence that the conventional rectangular building had its interior lightened by small windows high up above the top of the recessed panelling of the façade of the building. In the lower part of the *serech* on the funerary stela

188

of King Uadji, these windows are plainly shown with their
delicate tracery of a design of two lotus flowers tied together
(Fig. 103). Windows with this design are shown in every detailed portrayal of this form of architecture, and – to return
to the question of the Mesopotamian connexion – it is important to note that similar floral tracery is shown in what
appear to be window niches in representations of buildings
of the Jemdet Nasr period on the Euphrates (Fig. 110).
Windows set high on the walls are also plainly shown in the
model of a house of the First Dynasty
found at El Amra. In the decorative
embellishment of their buildings, these
early architects showed a taste and re-
finement which is astonishing. On the
completion of the structure the outside
was faced first with a thick mud plaster
laid on about 2 cm. thick. When dry,
this surface was covered by a thick
layer of gypsum plaster which in turn
was covered with a white lime wash.
This formed the ground for the painter, who covered it with intricate designs representing hanging matwork,
in black, red, yellow, blue, and green. Before the designs were
actually painted they were drawn in, in red, on the white
ground of the wall surface, and it is important to note that
guiding lines and proportion squares were made, as at the
present time, by plucking a stretched cord soaked in wet
paint, which was drawn tight across the surface of the wall.

Fig. 110. Façade of a
building of the Jemdet
Nasr period

The interior walls of corridors were usually painted a plain
white or yellow, but they frequently had a painted dado rail,
sometimes red and sometimes black. The paints used were
all made from powdered mineral substances applied with
water and probably gum, and, as has been pointed out, these

paints are really distempers. The artists' brushes were made from thin reed sticks hammered at one end so that the fibres separated to form bristles.

The walls of important rooms often had coloured reed mats stuck to them in the manner of modern wallpaper. In other cases the walls were lined with shallow pilasters encased in wood and in one example at least this wooden casing was inlaid with strips of gold plate embossed with the conventional bound reed pattern (Fig. 111).

Although Egyptian architecture in the Archaic Period has a distinctive character not found elsewhere, the rate of progress and some points of style are comparable with develop-

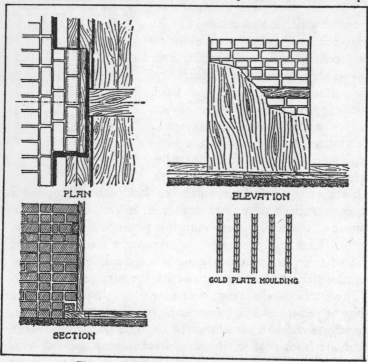

Fig. 111. Detail of wood-encased pilasters

ments which were occurring in contemporary Mesopotamia of the Jemdet Nasr period. Egypt was ahead of the Euphrates valley in the incipient use of dressed stone, but painted and recessed walls and the use of timber on façades are to some extent comparable, and undoubtedly had a common origin.

Chapter 7

LANGUAGE

OUR knowledge of the language of archaic Egypt can only be described as elementary, for at the present stage of our research the material available for study by the philologist is extremely limited. Nevertheless the pick of the excavator is yearly providing fresh material, and already evidence has been obtained which shows that the written language was by no means in its infancy, even at the beginning of the First Dynasty.

Even the earliest texts show that the written language had gone beyond the use of purely word signs which were pictures of objects or actions. There were also signs used to represent sounds only, and a system of numerical signs had also been evolved. Apart from the fact that the hieroglyphs are already stylistic and conventionalized, a cursive script was already in common use. All this shows that the written language must have had a considerable period of development behind it, of which no trace has as yet been found in Egypt. Some authorities point out that, given sufficient impetus, a written language can develop very rapidly; nevertheless one would expect to find some evidence of this development even though it took place during a limited period. It is, of course, possible that writing evolved in Lower Egypt which, as previously explained, is a closed book as regards the Archaic Period. But here again we would expect to find some evidence of it in the South during Predynastic times. Therefore until evidence to the contrary is forthcoming we must accept the fact that concurrent with the appearance of a highly developed monumental architecture, there is a fully developed system of writing. Let us now review the sources and type of objects which yield inscribed material.

MONUMENTAL INSCRIPTIONS

These can be divided into three categories: royal stelae, private stelae, and inscriptions on building material. The royal stelae were all found at Abydos and all take the same form: a stone slab, sometimes framed, within which is the name of the king (Fig. 48). The small private stelae found in the graves of retainers which surround the royal tombs at Abydos, although of crude workmanship, are more informative; for beside the name of the owner there are frequently titles given. Fig. 25 shows some typical examples of these objects.

Only two stelae of noblemen of the First Dynasty have been found, one from Abydos and the other from Sakkara, both dating to the reign of Ka'a, the last king of the dynasty. The Abydos stela belonged to Sabef, a companion in the royal palace, and the one from Sakkara belonged to Merka, a Sem priest (Pl. 30a). The texts on these two monuments are the most highly developed yet found, and we find on them for the first time linguistic formulae which became stereotyped in later times.

In the Second Dynasty, private stelae developed along conventional lines and are rich in written material (Pl. 32a); and at the end of this period, in the reign of Kha-sekhemui, inscribed blocks and a door jamb found at Hieraconpolis and El Kab have hieroglyphic forms which are almost indistinguishable from those of the succeeding pyramid period.

LABELS

The most important sources of written historical material, as
far as the First Dynasty is concerned, are small wooden and
ivory labels which were attached to objects and stores placed
in the tombs. The small labels, varying in size from 1 × 1.2
cm. to 7.5 × 9.5 cm., are sometimes engraved and sometimes
painted in black and red; but all bear texts relative to the
commodity to which they were attached, such as its name
and quantity. But above all, the larger labels frequently record the most important event of one year of a king's reign,
this being the established method of marking the date of the
record. Like the yearly records on the Palermo Stone, many
of the labels, particularly those dated to the latter half of the
First Dynasty, have their text preceded by the year sign.
Although these historical texts cannot as yet be deciphered
with any certainty, in many cases the gist of their meaning
can be ascertained. Other labels give merely the name and
quantity of the commodity to which they were attached, but
even these short texts are invaluable material for study. Fig.
112 shows typical examples of these labels.

Fig. 112. Examples of wood and ivory labels

JAR-SEALINGS

But the richest source of inscribed material is contained in
the seal impressions which mark the lumps of clay which
cover the mouths of wine and food jars (Figs. 113, 114, and
115). These impressions were made by engraved cylinders

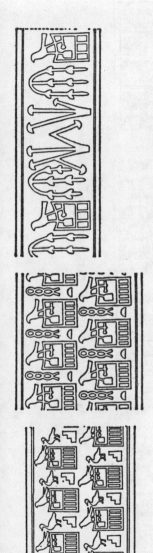

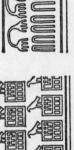

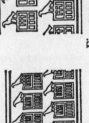

Fig. 113. Examples of jar-sealings of the early First Dynasty

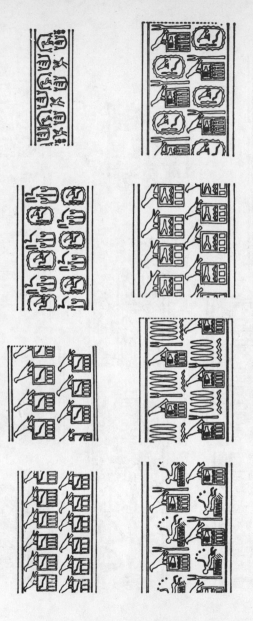

Fig. 114. Examples of jar-sealings of the middle First Dynasty

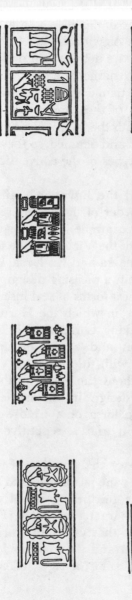

Fig. 115. Examples of jar-sealings of the late First Dynasty and Second Dynasty

of wood or stone run over the damp clay, so that the design is repeated again and again. As with the labels the texts on these impressions in many cases defy certain decipherment, but as they principally refer to names and titles, considerable progress has been made, particularly with regard to calligraphy; for in the engraving of these important objects far more care was taken than with the labels. Consequently the signs are usually well formed and detailed, so they can easily be recognized as the prototypes of the conventional hieroglyphs of later times.

Even at this early period the Egyptian craftsman had adopted the rule that the order of signs must give way to the symmetry of design; for example, on the seal shown in Fig. 116 we have the name of the Vizier written alternately

Fig. 116. Jar-sealing of the Vizier Hemaka

H-ma-ka and Ka-h-ma, in order to obtain a pleasing design. The commonest forms of seal inscription are those in which the Horus name of the king is repeated in two rows, again and again, or in a single row with titles between each *serech*. This form continues throughout the whole of the Archaic Period. Another common design in the earlier part of the First Dynasty takes the form of a trelliswork shrine with a lioness in front of it and a repetitive group of signs.

During the Second Dynasty the practice of impressing the clay sealings of food and wine jars appears to have diminished, and in consequence the period is not as rich in inscribed material of this character as is the First Dynasty. But the seal impressions that we do find are superior both in design and execution and show a rapid move towards the conventional grouping of signs of subsequent periods.

INSCRIPTIONS ON STONE AND POTTERY VESSELS

Other important sources of inscribed material are the texts that we find on stone and pottery vessels. These may be summarily classed as follows:

1. *Incised texts on stone vessels* (Fig. 117). These nearly always refer to names and titles and less frequently to an event such as a Sed festival or to a place such as a royal tomb or palace. In general, texts of this class would appear to be made to mark the ownership of the vessel or the place to which it belonged.

Fig. 117. Examples of incised writing on stone vessels

However, this explanation is not entirely satisfactory; we have, for example, a specimen with two or three royal names inscribed by the same hand. In the early part of the First Dynasty such inscriptions are crudely executed and short; but the practice of marking stone vessels in this way came more and more into favour, and by the time of the Second Dynasty we find such texts carefully inscribed with well-formed signs.

2. *Painted texts on stone vessels* (Fig. 118). These are not as common as the inscribed texts, and are usually done in black ink with a fairly thick brush. Here again, they consist mainly of names and titles denoting ownership. Their cursive character shows a long familiarity with a system of rapid writing.

3. *Incised texts on pottery vessels executed before firing* (Fig. 119). These are not to be confused with pot marks, which we will discuss later, for they are true hieroglyphs although crudely formed. Although hundreds of specimens have been found, they nearly all belong to the reigns of two First Dynasty kings, Enezib and Semerkhet. That of Enezib consists of the stepped structure with a group of signs within it, and those of Semerkhet consists of his Horus name within a crenellated oval or fortified enclosure. It would appear that the inscriptions are place names and were marked by the potter to indicate the building, palace, or tomb for which the vessel was intended.

Fig. 118. Examples of painted writing on stone vessels

4. *Painted texts on pottery vessels* (Fig. 120). These texts, written in cursive hieroglyphs, usually give the name of the owner and the contents of the jar. Specimens of this class of inscribed material have been found which date prior to the First Dynasty, in the reigns of Ka'a and Narmer. During the First Dynasty, such inscriptions are always made with black ink, but in the Second Dynasty white paint was commonly used.

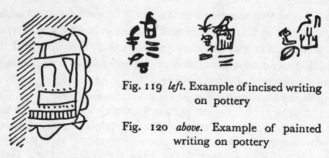

Fig. 119 *left*. Example of incised writing on pottery

Fig. 120 *above*. Example of painted writing on pottery

INSCRIPTIONS ON OTHER OBJECTS

Apart from inscribed material found on stone monuments, labels, jar-sealings, and pottery and stone vessels, other objects such as toilet implements, gaming pieces, tools, etc., are sometimes inscribed with short texts like the lid of the seal box of King Udimu which gives his name and explains its contents. From all these sources we can now list 203 hieroglyphs which were in common use in later times.

POT MARKS

We now come to the pot marks or what has been aptly called a signary – signs entirely disconnected with known hieroglyphs, which are found on the great wine jars of the First and Second Dynasties (Fig. 121). These signs were made by a sharp instrument on the pots before they were fired and their purpose is still a matter of debate. They are certainly not haphazard marks, but follow some form of ordered grouping, and they have been variously described as owners' marks, potters' signatures, indications of the future contents of the vessel, etc.; but none of these explanations is entirely satisfactory. They cannot have been owners' marks or potters' signatures, for the same groups of signs have been noted on pots whose dates of manufacture are divided by a span of more than a hundred years. It is just possible that the marks indicate the workshop in which the pot was made; but even this would not appear very probable, for we get different groups of signs on vessels which certainly come from the same source, shown by the identity in form and texture of the clay. One thing is certain: the system of marking was not confined to one locality but was in use all over Egypt. Furthermore, it was not confined to a limited period, for we find the same groups in use for more than three hundred years.

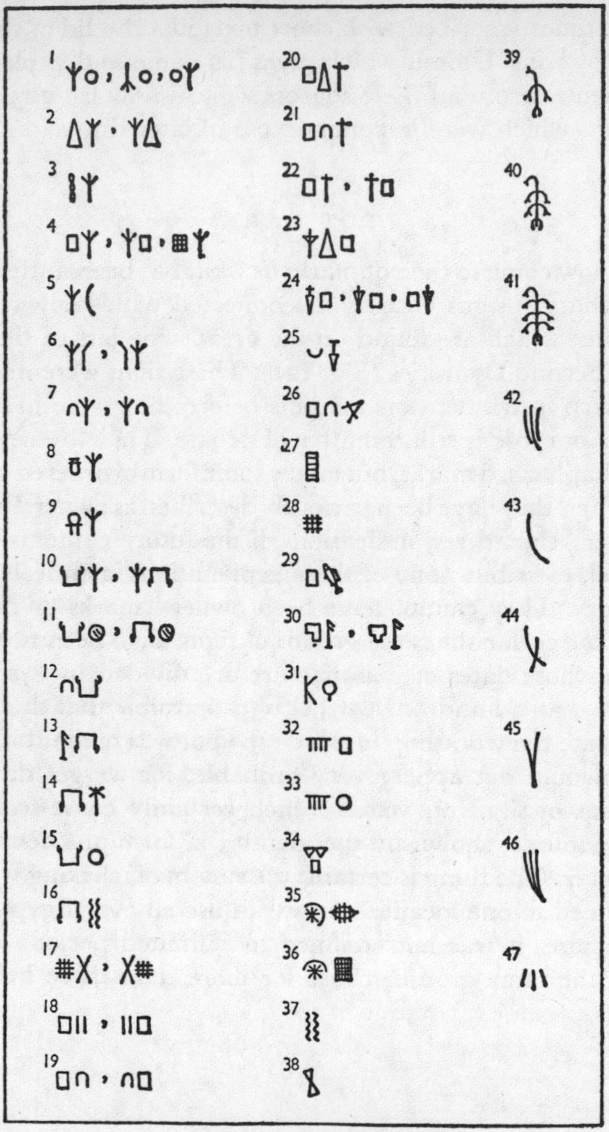

Fig. 121. Pot marks

Chapter 8

TRADE

IMPORTS

There is ample evidence of well-organized internal trade in Egypt during the Archaic Period, and an examination of non-Egyptian materials shows that the exchange of goods with her foreign neighbours was extensive even in the earliest times.

Some conception of the ramifications of the internal trade is gained when we consider the place of origin of natural materials found in such widely separated centres as Sakkara, Abydos, and Hieraconpolis. For example, in the important industry of stone vessel manufacture, alabaster probably came from Hat-nub in the Eastern Desert and from an area behind Helwan; basalt from the Fayum; diorite from the Eastern Desert, Aswan, and a special variety of this stone from an area forty miles north-west of Abu Simbel in Nubia; breccia from areas in the Western Desert between Minia and Esna; dolomite from the Eastern Desert; schist and volcanic ash from the Wadi-el-Hammamat; marble and porphyritic rock from the Red Sea coast area; purple porphyry from Gebel Dokhan in the Eastern Desert; serpentine and rock crystal from the Eastern Desert.

The wide distribution of pottery is shown by the pot marks, identical signs made by the same hand being found in different archaic sites throughout the country. Although in building it was usual to use local stone, the transfer of stone from areas far afield was not unknown, such as the granite from

Aswan which was used in the tomb of Udimu at Abydos. Fragments of Aswan granite have also been found in the ruins of the Archaic Period at Sakkara. In transporting the produce of the quarries overland, the early Egyptians must have used sledges, for the cart was unknown to them, though its use had been discovered by their contemporaries in Mesopotamia. Once it was on the banks of the Nile, the stone could easily be transported to its destination, for all important centres were within easy reach of the river.

Of areas outside Egypt proper, Sinai was a source of various raw materials, the most important of which were copper, malachite, and turquoise. At this early period, foreign imports, although limited in number, were indispensable, particularly timber for building purposes. Undoubtedly a great lumber trade already existed in the First Dynasty, for the architects and boat builders depended on the import of considerable quantities of cedar and cypress from Lebanon and Syria. Ebony, used in the embellishment of furniture, was also imported from the far south, whence a certain amount of elephant ivory was also obtained. Other important materials of foreign origin were obsidian and lapis-lazuli from western Asia and resin from the far south.

Another import of particular interest to the archaeologist was a certain class of pottery vessels of undoubted foreign manufacture which were in common use during the latter half of the First Dynasty. These vessels, of flask-like form, are probably of north Syrian origin and perhaps found their way to Egypt as containers of olive oil or other exported commodities. They have been found at Byblos, the Syrian port of export to Egypt; but as Egyptian pottery of the same period has also been found there, they themselves might be an import into Syria. But on balance it would appear likely that they originated in this area.

EXPORTS

We know little of Egypt's exports, but her stone vessels have been found in Byblos, Palestine, Crete, and even on the Greek mainland at Mycenae and Asine. So that, by the time of the Second Dynasty, as well as raw materials, Egypt was exporting the products of her craftsmen to distant lands. The trade routes were probably the same as in later times: by sea to Byblos for the Syrian trade; by the El Auja road across north Sinai for Palestine; through the Wadi-el-Tumilat to south Sinai; through the Wadi-el-Hammamat to the Red Sea and thence south to the Somaliland and Arabian coasts; and finally by the Nile to the Sudan.

TRANSPORT

We do not know if the sea traffic was carried by Egyptian ships or by foreign traders, but, as it is obvious that large vessels sailed the Nile in their internal trade, there is no reason to suppose that the Egyptians were incapable of building sea-going ships and of navigating them.

Chapter 9

INDUSTRY

POTTERY

One of the most important industries was the manufacture of pottery. But unlike the craft in later times, it gave no place to the artist and was strictly utilitarian in character. Throughout the period the artist's attention was directed to the stone vessels, and it was only with the decay of this industry in the pyramid age that pottery became a vehicle for aesthetic expression. But, unconsciously, the artistic genius of the Egyptian showed even in the mass-produced earthenware, and the forms of some classes of pottery vessels are truly delightful in their simplicity and balance. That this was realized on occasion by the artist is shown by the deliberate copying of humble pottery forms in vessels of alabaster, schist, and volcanic ash.

There was a long history of pottery production behind the industry at the time of the Unification, but although there were certain survivals in design, a new and distinctive earthenware made its appearance just prior to the First Dynasty. The black-topped, incised, and painted decorative pottery of the Late Predynastic period disappeared and the wavy-handle motif only survived for a very limited period. It is significant that the black-topped and incised decorative pottery continued in Nubia for many more hundreds of years, but north of the natural frontier of the First Cataract new forms and new techniques were established, contemporary with the advent of monumental architecture, and so on.

Egypt is rich in its clays, which may be divided into two distinct varieties: one of blackish colour which becomes brown or red when baked; and the other brownish-grey which turns to a grey-buff when baked. This latter clay is confined to limited areas in Upper Egypt and was not used by the potter during the Archaic Period, for the mass of earthenware of all types is brownish-red.

The categorical statements of some authorities that the wheel was not known in the First and Second Dynasties is incorrect. Although the use of the wheel was by no means universal, it was nevertheless widely used and pottery formed on a slow hand-turned wheel is fairly common.

With regard to baking, we have no evidence of pottery kilns, although they may well have existed. Otherwise the usual primitive method of baking a mixed pile of pots and fuel must have been followed. But considering the vast output of the potter at this time, such primitive methods would appear inadequate and some simple method of separating the pottery from the burning fuel was certainly in existence.

Fig. 122 shows a representative group of the various classes of pottery in common use during the First and Second Dynasties, and although we are uncertain of the functions of some of them, in general we are able to distinguish between vessels for storage and vessels for eating purposes. Indeed, with regard to the former, in many cases we know the character of the commodity which they were made to contain. This knowledge has come to us largely through the recent excavations at Sakkara, where the state of preservation of foodstuffs and other materials is remarkable, as for example the Second Dynasty funerary repast described on page 243.

The big jars of Class 1 contained wine and great quantities of them were stored in the magazines of all the big tombs, as shown in Plate 20. They vary in size according to period, the larger and fatter type at the beginning of the First Dynasty

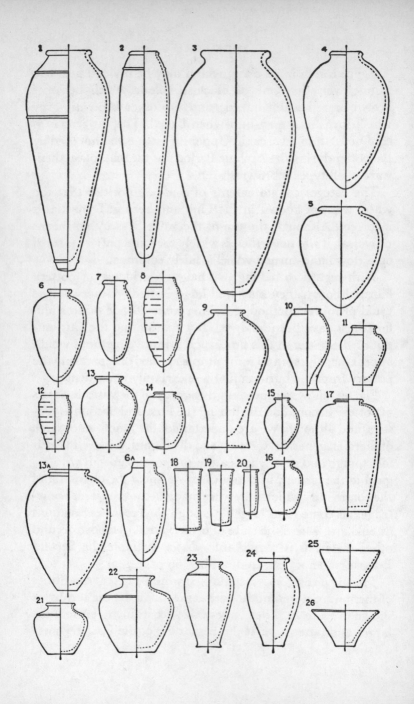

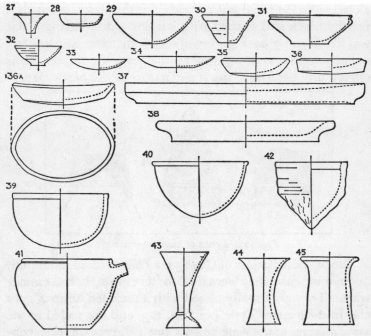

Fig. 122 (opposite and above). Types of pottery vessels

becoming smaller and more slender until it takes the form of Class 2. The method of sealing these big wine jars was to place a round saucer-like cap in an inverted position over the mouth. Covering this and reaching to the shoulders was a large lump of yellow clay modelled into a cone-shaped form as shown on Fig. 123. Over this clay cap a wooden or stone cylinder seal was rolled up one side and down the other. Sometimes a second seal was rolled at right angles to the first, both impressions crossing near the top. As explained in Chapter 7, it is on the sealings of these wine jars that we depend to a large extent to ascertain the identity of the owners of many of the big tombs. This method of sealing applies only to the First Dynasty. Wine jars of Class 2 are

209

closed with the usual pottery cap, but the clay covering it is
usually black and shaped with straight sides, having a flat
top like Type 3 on Fig. 123. Jars of this class are less frequently sealed, and, even when they are, the impression is
often faulty because of the sticky nature of the black clay.

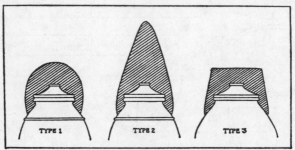

Fig. 123. Types of clay jar-sealings

The big bulbous jars of Class 3 may have contained liquid,
but in some cases they were used to store grain such as emmer
wheat. They are usually closed with a rounded lump of grey
clay in the form of Type I on Fig. 123, and are sealed in the
same manner as the wine jars of Class I. Jars of this class continued in common use until the end of the First Dynasty, but
they are very rare at any later date, and when found they
appear to have belonged to the earlier period and to have
been re-used.

Jars of Classes 4, 5, and 6 were apparently used for the
storage of food of a cereal character, and in one large First
Dynasty tomb at Sakkara sixty-seven of Class 6 were found
to contain the remains of small loaves of bread. They are
usually sealed with conical-shaped clay sealings, uninscribed,
and are sometimes covered with a white lime wash. The form
of Class 4 continues well into the Second Dynasty. Class 6A
is a form confined entirely to the Second Dynasty, and even
then was not very common. No evidence has been found regarding its contents, but it was probably used for the storage

of food. The small jar of Class 7 was very common in the First Dynasty, but did not survive the end of this period. These jars are frequently inscribed in black ink with the name of the owner and the commodity which they contained, perhaps an oil.

Very large quantities of jars of Class 8 are found on all First Dynasty sites. It is a crude hand-made pot of coarse brown clay and it appears to have been of general utility and on occasion has been found to contain cereals, fruit, and even meat bones.

Large jars of Class 9 are of coarse brown ware with a thin red slip. They occur only in the first half of the First Dynasty and no indication of their purpose has yet been found.

Classes 10 and 11 are common forms and are probably the prototype of Classes 21, 22, and 23 of the Second Dynasty. Small versions of Class 11 have been sometimes found to contain fruit.

Like Class 8, Class 12 is a crude hand-made pot of general utility confined to the period of the early First Dynasty. Many jars of this type were found in the grave of a servant of Queen Meryet-nit at Sakkara. His profession was obvious, for all the jars contained red, green, and yellow paint. But in other circumstances they have been used in the storage of wheat and small loaves of bread.

Jars of Classes 13 and 13A are remarkable for the care taken in their manufacture. Most of the archaic pottery, although attractive in form, is crudely made, but these jars are usually finely shaped, with a thin red slip and pebble polish. They are fairly common throughout the First Dynasty, but do not survive into the Second. There is no evidence regarding their purpose, but as they are sometimes found in a group with eating vessels, it is possible that they were used for wine or water during the repast. In support of this, it must be noted that they have never been found sealed with clay and they have been copied in beaten copper (see Metal-work).

Classes 14, 15, and 16 are of similar fabric to the larger jars of 13 and 13A and are of the same careful manufacture. In common use in the early First Dynasty, they continued to survive until the end of the Second Dynasty almost unchanged in form and size. With flat disk lids, they were used to contain fruit. The large jar of Class 17, exclusive to the Second Dynasty, is also of careful manufacture. Although large numbers of this class have been found, there is no evidence of its use.

The tubular jars of Classes 18, 19, and 20 were used, to judge from chemical analysis, as containers of cheese, and have been found in great quantities in the tombs of the first half of the First Dynasty; Class 18, of buff ware, is dated to the reigns of Narmer and Hor-aha, no fewer than 200 being found in the latter's tomb at Sakkara. They are always inscribed in black ink with the name of the owner and the contents. Class 19, still buff ware but smaller, is dated to Uadji, and is not inscribed. The very small variety of Class 20, dated to Udimu, is of red ware and uninscribed.

Classes 21, 22, and 23 are exclusive to the Second Dynasty. They are never found sealed, but they are frequently capped with a small shallow chalice-shaped cup, inverted, and in this way they are frequently depicted on monuments of the period. Made of a rough brown ware, the body of the jar is painted with a red wash and the rim, neck, and shoulders painted black.

Jars of Class 24 also belong to the period of the Second Dynasty. They are not very common and we have no evidence of their purpose.

Rough brown ware bowls of Class 25 were common in the early part of the First Dynasty, but are rare after the reign of Udimu.

Although not very common, bowls of Classes 26 and 27 (Fig. 122) continued throughout the First and Second Dynasties.

Bowls and dishes of Classes 28 to 36 were all used as eating vessels. Made of rough red-brown ware, they are usually painted with a red wash which did not survive when the vessels were heated to serve cooked foods. The big flat dishes of Classes 37 and 38, made of the same rough clay, were also used to contain hot food. Such bowls and dishes continued in common use throughout the whole of the Archaic Period. The bowls with the rounded base, Classes 39 and 40, are dated only to the Second Dynasty, as is the spouted bowl of Class 41.

Class 42 is a very roughly made bowl with a conical base. This type of vessel is far more common during the Second Dynasty, but it was in use during the earliest times. Hundreds of these bowls were found in a large Second Dynasty tomb at Sakkara and fully half of them were unbaked. There is at present no satisfactory explanation of the use to which they were put, although it has been suggested, and accepted by some authorities, that they were used for baking bread. They continued in common use until well into the Pyramid Age.

Although, as previously stated, pottery was manufactured almost entirely for a utilitarian purpose, we find occasionally that a craftsman designs in clay a vessel which goes beyond this and is obviously an attempt to copy in his humble medium the attractive designs of the artist in stone vases. Such a form is that of Class 43, dated to the early part of the First Dynasty.

Pottery vessels with pointed bases were intended to stand in sand or the rough earth floor, but the hard flooring of better class dwellings necessitated some form of support. This was supplied by the potter in the form of hollow pedestals such as those of Classes 44 and 45 which continued in common use throughout the whole period.

The potter did not confine his skill solely to the manufacture of jars, bowls, dishes, and cups; he produced other necessities for which his medium was suitable. Big cylindrical granaries, sometimes more than a metre high, were made of pottery. These had a circular opening at the top to pour in the grain and a rectangular door at the bottom through which it could be withdrawn as wanted. The potter also made the big caps for the openings of built-in grain bins such as are shown in Fig. 140. Other objects manufactured by the potter were models of houses, granaries, and boats for the equipment of tombs.

STONE VESSELS (FIGURE 125)

The stone vessels of the archaic Egyptians were perhaps their greatest vehicle for artistic expression, and no country then or since has achieved such perfection as did this ancient industry in its effort to produce an object of utility which was also a thing of beauty. They were made in such vast quantities that the quality varies, but even so the proportion of aesthetic triumphs in design and technique is astonishing.

No stone – with the exception of granite – was too hard to use, and specimens dated to the First and Second Dynasties have been found which are made of the following: diorite, schist, alabaster, volcanic ash, serpentine, steatite, breccia, marble, limestone, mottled black and white porphyritic rock, purple porphyry, red jasper, obsidian quartz, dolomite, rock crystal, and basalt.

Unfortunately, we have no really satisfactory evidence of the method of manufacture of these stone vessels, and, although certain processes of the work are known to us, others remain a complete mystery. How did they achieve such accuracy that when we 'swing' a shallow bowl or dish, no deviation from a perfect circle can be noted? How did they cut rock crystal tubular jars with walls not more than a millimetre thick? Although we have no evidence, it would appear almost certain that the craftsman had some method of rotating the material against a fixed tool, for it would be impossible to obtain such accuracy purely by hand chiselling and grinding by measurements, no matter how numerous or how painstakingly done.

From unfinished vessels we have ascertained that the vessel was finished externally before the hollowing of the interior was begun. We know also that the rough cutting of the interior was done with the aid of a drill with a curious eccentric handle, to which two oval stones were slung with ropes. These stone weights, which splayed outwards when the drill was turned, thus provided extra motive power. The cutting head of these drills was a flint blade shaped rather like a blunt arrow-head. Such drill-heads, and stone weights, have been found in considerable quantity, and we also have pictures of the Pyramid Age which show the drill being worked (Fig. 124). A tubular drill was also used for work on smaller vessels. But this method of drilling, while adequate for cutting the interior of cylindrical vases, such as Types 1 to 22 shown on Fig. 125, would not be practical for hollowing out the inside of the jars of Types 23 to 24. How, for example, was the upward pressure obtained to cut away the interior side of the shoulders? All these problems as yet remain unanswered and are likely to remain so until perhaps the discovery of a stone vase maker's workshop which will reveal some of his methods.

Both flint and copper tools were used and in the divisions between the leaves of the schist bowl shown on Plate 39A, we have indeed found the marks of a copper saw.

Fig. 124. An Old Kingdom representation of stone vessel manufacture

WOODWORK

The craft of the woodworker only effectively came into existence at the end of the Predynastic period, when the manufacture of copper tools was well established. This being the case, it is astonishing that early in the First Dynasty, objects of the carpenters' and joiners' crafts give ample evidence of an advanced knowledge of working in wood. All the principles of jointing, such as both stump and through tenon tongued, rebate, half lap, and dovetail were known and used; moreover, elaborate carving and inlay of mixed woods with ivory and faience were a commonplace. Although their tools were few in number, they nevertheless fulfilled all the essential functions of modern carpentry, with the exception of the plane, which remained an unknown implement in

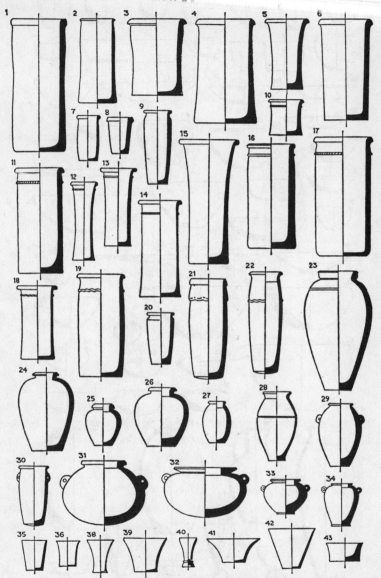

Fig. 125 (above and overleaf). Types of stone vessels

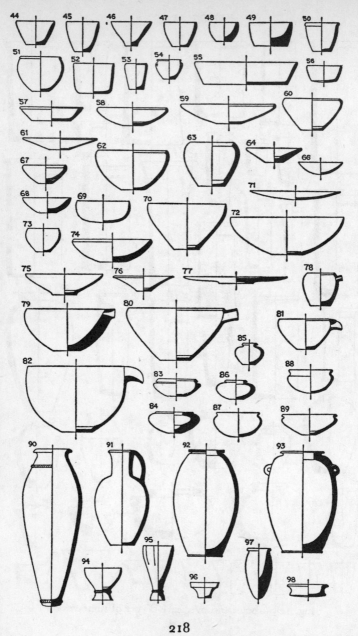

Egypt until Roman times. It is interesting to note that the form of these tools remained, in general, the same throughout ancient Egypt's history and that the archaic woodworker's favourite tool, the adze, often used as a plane, is still the most important item of his modern descendant's equipment. The adzes (Fig. 126) vary considerably in size: some have a copper blade 12 cm. in length attached to a wooden haft about 30 cm. long, while others have a blade 28 cm. long and a heavy haft 78 cm. in length. The blade is attached to the haft with a binding of cord or leather thongs.

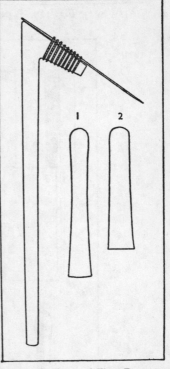

The saw (Fig. 127) also varies in size with a blade from 13 to 40 cm. in length. Only one edge is serrated, but not always along its entire length; the teeth, about 1 mm. long, begin a short distance from the shoulder and end before the tip is reached. The blade is socketed into a straight wooden handle. Unlike the modern tool, the saw was pulled and not pushed, so that the cutting edge of the teeth is set towards the handle.

Fig. 126. Type of First Dynasty adze

There was a considerable variety of chisels ranging from a heavy type about 30 cm. long to small delicate engraving tools. The four main types are shown on Fig. 128. Obviously the chisels fitted with rounded-top handles were used for hand work and the flat-topped for light hammer work.

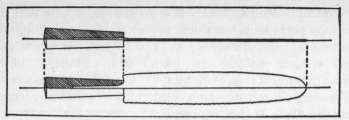

Fig. 127. Type of First Dynasty saw

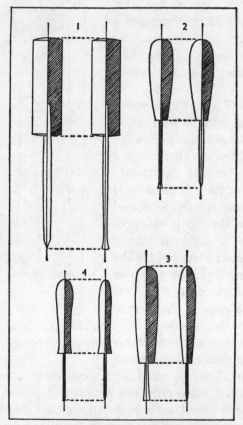

Fig. 128. Types of First Dynasty chisels

Although no carpenters' hammers of the Archaic Period have as yet been found, it is probable that they were of the wooden club-like variety used in later times. Heavy stone hammers have been found at Helwan, but these were probably used in masonry and not in woodwork.

Copper awls or piercers of the type shown in Fig. 129 were used by both the carpenter and the leather-worker. Although

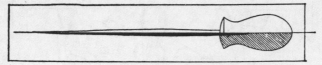

Fig. 129. Type of First Dynasty awl

actual specimens have not been found, it would appear almost certain that the bow drill was used in the making of holes for wooden nails. It is uncertain if some method of turning was employed, for the accuracy of parts of wooden furniture, circular in section, is such that it sometimes appears to have been impossible of achievement by hand-work alone. But in the absence of any evidence the question must be left unanswered at present.

The bevelling and rounding of edges clearly show the marks of a knife used in the manner of a spoke-shave, and the application of a knife in this way may explain the extraordinary smoothness of flat surfaces which could not have been achieved entirely with stone rubbing.

Although in jointing the tenon and mortice, reinforced by a wooden peg, was nearly always used, in the case of bed, chair, and table legs we frequently find the survival of older methods, such as a binding with leather thongs, being still used even when the joint has already been made by the former method (Fig. 130). While wooden pegs and dowels were favoured, the use of big copper nails was not unknown, as well as small copper tacks for attaching leather upholstery

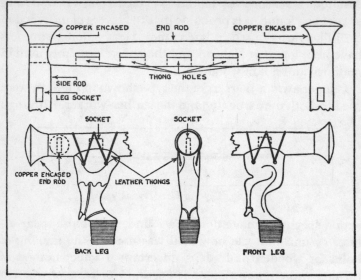

Fig. 130. Construction details of a wooden bed

and copper fittings such as the terminals on bed and chair rods. Inlay, whether of wood, ivory, or faience, was always fastened with glue.

WEAVING

The manufacture of linen was already highly developed early in the First Dynasty and experts who have examined specimens from Abydos, Sakkara, and Tarkhan consider that, apart from the irregularity in the spacing of the warp threads, the ancient craftsmen practised all the methods of plain weaving that are known today. Moreover, examination of the fibres of the best linen of the period frequently shows that it was made of a finer flax than the best modern qualities. It also shows that the processing of flax was the same as that of today: the strong resin which binds the fibre to the straw was removed by the putrefactive operation known as 'retting', and the 'heckling' or separating was just as efficiently achieved.

We have no direct evidence of the type of loom used, but judging from its products it must have been an efficient machine at a comparatively late stage in the volution of its design, similar in character to those figured on the tomb paintings of later periods. All the fabrics show the same type of weaving, known in Lancashire as the 'calico-weave' – that is, a simple one up and one down. They vary considerably in texture, some being of the coarseness of sacking while others, like that found in the tomb of Zer at Abydos, rival modern cambric, with 160 threads to the inch in the warp and 120 in the woof.

Flax was also used in the manufacture of rope, the finest example of which was found at Sakkara. This rope, almost perfectly preserved, had a circumference of 3 cm. and was made up of three strands consisting of approximately 190 yarns per strand. Thin cord or string was also made from flax; but heavy rope for hauling appears to have been more usually made with fibre.

The manufacture of reed and grass mats has always been an important industry in Egypt, but in archaic times it must have been most extensively practised, for matting was used widely in architecture and domestic furnishing. Some conception of its importance can be gained from its influence in decorative art. The mat motif is more common than any other in painted decoration, ivory, and wood carving (Figs. 98 and 99). Light mats are usually formed by flat grass plaits darned through a flax string warp, while the heavy type consists of twisted grass strands darned through a more or less rigid reed warp. Judging from the similarity of the ancient matting to that made in Egypt at the present time, it would appear probable that the structure of the loom and method of work was the same: that is, with the loom pegged out on the ground, the operator moving forward in a squatting posture on the mat itself as it takes form. The variety of pattern design may be judged from the painted copies of mats on the panelled walls of the tomb. There is evidence to show that mats were used to form the walls of wooden framework buildings, as floor coverings, and as wall decoration (see p. 190).

Basketry was another industry of major importance, and this type of receptacle varies from small circular food baskets made of plaited strips of palm leaf to big rectangular chests measuring nearly a metre in length. Basket-work chests of this size are usually made with thick reed or strips of palm branches.

METAL-WORK

The only metals known and worked by the archaic Egyptians were gold and copper; the former being used almost exclusively in jewellery and to a limited extent in architectural embellishment; the latter in the making of tools, weapons, and vessels.

Copper was known in the Predynastic period but only used to a very limited extent in the making of small implements and jewellery. It was not until the period of the Unification that it was employed in the extensive manufacture of tools and weapons and household utensils (Figs. 131 and 132). It has been suggested, but not proved, that the small copper implements of the predynastic people were made from the metal found in the metallic state and that they were ignorant of the knowledge of obtaining it by the smelting of ores. Certainly the acquisition of this knowledge would explain the sudden advent of Egypt's copper age, just prior to the foundation of the First Dynasty, for after that date all the metal was derived from ore mined in the Eastern Desert and Sinai. This ore was of course smelted in the locality in which it was found

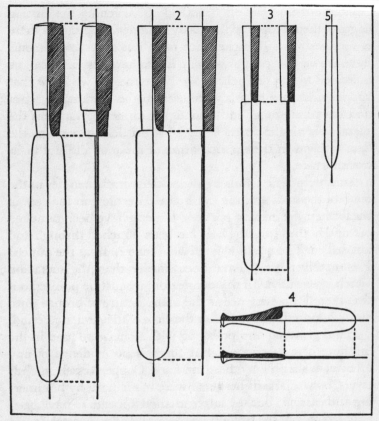

Fig. 131. Types of copper knives with wooden handles

and the resultant copper transported to the workshops in the
Nile valley. In shaping the metal, hammering cold and hot
and moulding were practised, and in the manufacture of tools
we find examples of each method, and sometimes a combination of both. In the case of light tools, such as knives and saw
blades, the metal was cut roughly to shape and then cold-
hammered. Heavier tools, such as adze, axe, and hoe blades,
appear to have been cast roughly to shape and then hammered while still hot from the mould. Authorities have

225

pointed out that the only method of hardening the cutting edges of their copper tools was by hammering and that there is no question of the existence of a 'lost art'. Experiments have shown that copper with an initial hardness of 87 can be increased to 135 (Brinell scale) Nevertheless, we know that copper saws and chisels were used in the working of schist and hard limestone, and although hammering hardens the metal it is also inclined to make it brittle. So perhaps the 'lost art' was in the manipulation of the tool and not in its manufacture.

Another puzzle left us by the ancient craftsmen lies in the teeth of the saws and the eye-holes of needles; in the case of the former, the missing portions of metal have been punched out and in the latter the hole has been punched through and not drilled. The question is: of what material was the punch? Presumably it must have been harder than the metal on which it was used. In this connexion, it must be pointed out that there is no evidence of the manufacture of bronze until many hundreds of years after the close of the Archaic Period.

Hand grinding and polishing with stone were used in the finishing of copper tools, but there is no evidence of any attempt at shaping by these methods. Copper vessels, such as ewers, bowls, jars, dishes, etc., were made both by hammering and casting; but the latter method appears to have been adopted only in the Second Dynasty and all the vessels found in the tomb of Zer at Sakkara were made of hammered copper (Pl. 43). The spouts of ewers, handles, and rims were attached with copper rivets. Binding with wire was also used in the fixing of loop handles such as that on No. 3 in Fig. 132, a fact that is of considerable interest, for until the discovery of this vessel it was believed that wire drawing was unknown to these early metal-workers. Nearly all the forms of copper vessels were copied from stone prototypes and the metalworker appears to have exercised little originality in design.

However, he did apparently appreciate some of the possibilities of his medium, as for example the introduction of the looped handle over the top of a vessel, a feature unachieved at that time in stone or pottery.

Both nugget and alluvial gold are found in Egypt and Nubia, but since the extraction of the metal from sand and gravel is easier than mining in hard quartz rock, it is probable

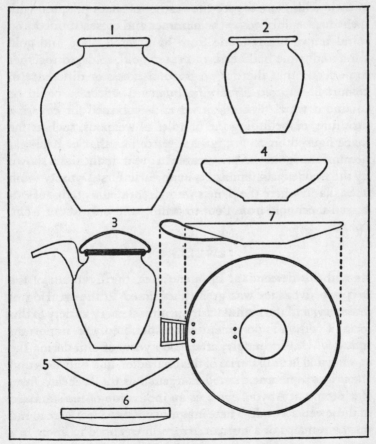

Fig. 132. Examples of copper vessels

that the early Egyptians largely depended on the alluvial deposits for their supply of the precious metal. Since nugget gold has also been found in archaic tombs, this source must have been known to them as it was to their successors.

The goldsmiths both cast and hammered the metal, and the magnificent jewellery found in the tomb of Zer at Abydos and in the tomb of Her-nit at Sakkara shows the high degree of their skill. Here we see the casting of small plaques, with their surface finished by the hammer and chisel, tubular and spiral barrel beads made from hammered plate and gold wire, and triple ball beads of beaten gold, soldered together so perfectly that there is no trace of excess or difference in colour. Sheet gold of varying but even thickness could be produced which was engraved and embossed for covering furniture, embellishing the handles of weapons, such as the mace figured on p. 115, and sceptres like that of Kha-sek-hemui. That gold was procurable in great quantities is shown by the wooden cased pilasters in an early First Dynasty tomb at Sakkara, where the panels were decorated by strips of embossed sheet gold from floor to ceiling and only about 1 cm. apart.

JEWELLERY

As with his descendant of later times, the Egyptian of the first two dynasties was greatly addicted to the wearing of jewellery, and the manufacture of almost every variety of this form of personal adornment was undoubtedly an important industry. Unfortunately, after 5000 years of plundering the tombs yield little material of this character, and only now and then does some unexpected find, such as the bracelets from Zer's tomb at Abydos, give us an indication of the standard of the jeweller's craft. These magnificent bracelets were found on the remains of a human arm, still wrapped in linen, in a crevice in a wall of the tomb, where they had been left through the oversight of some ancient plunderers. It has been stated that the arm belonged to Zer's queen, but there is no evidence in support of this or even that the bones are female. But whoever their owner was, there can be no question that in this jewellery we have an example of the highest class of this form of personal adornment made in the early years of the First Dynasty. Fig. 133 shows the design of the four bracelets and the order of the materials: gold, turquoise, purple lazuli, and amethyst.

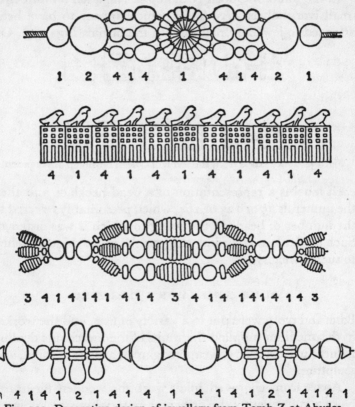

Fig. 133. Decorative design of jewellery from Tomb Z at Abydos.
1, gold; 2, amethyst; 3, lazuli; 4, turquoise

As in later times, intricate beadwork was favoured in the composition of necklaces and bracelets, although in the case of the latter, cast and beaten copper, shell, and ivory were common. In the manufacture of beads, apart from gold and faience, the following semi-precious stones were known and utilized by the archaic jeweller: agate, onyx, amethyst, cornelian, chalcedony, green felspar, garnet, haematite, jasper, lapis lazuli, malachite, rock crystal, and turquoise.

In the tomb of Queen Nithotep at Nagadeh a number of small ivory labels were found which appear to have been attached to jewellery placed with the burial (Fig. 134). On

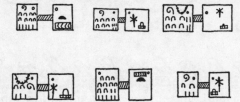

Fig. 134. Ivory labels from the tomb of Queen Nithotep at Nagadeh

each label is a representation of a bead necklace and then the numerals 75 or 123 or 164, which presumably referred to the number of beads in the string to which it was fastened. Such meticulous recording suggests the great value attached to such jewellery.

BONE AND IVORY CARVING

Bone and ivory were put to a variety of uses, and the worker in this medium supplied the wants of the merchants dealing in furniture, jewellery, weapons, games, articles of toilet, and sculpture.

Apart from engraved inlay work for wooden furniture, ivory was frequently the principal material in small objects, such as little tables and stools, where the common 'bull' legs are made entirely of it. Ivory and bone arrow-heads have been found in great quantities both at Abydos and Sakkara and we even have an example of a large ivory spear-head which appears to have been made from a natural tusk with a minimum of shaping. But it was in the manufacture of gaming pieces that the ivory carver could give full rein to his skill as an artist, particularly in the carving of the 'bull' legs of the board and the lions and dicing sticks (Pl. 48).

In sculpture, the most superb example is the ivory statuette of the aged king which is shown on Plate 30b; and of incised work there is nothing superior to the engraving of the name of Uadji on a fragment of a throwing-stick.

LEATHERWORK

Leatherwork was another important and indeed essential industry for this material was widely used in the making of bags, arrow quivers, wearing apparel, and furniture. Unfortunately, it is rare for leather to be found well preserved, but it is also rare to find that it has disappeared without trace; usually, even if the leather object crumbles at the touch, its character can be ascertained before its final disappearance. Thin leather such as was used in small bags often has the consistency of burnt cardboard, but the thicker variety used in footwear can often be preserved, and indeed in recent excavations at Sakkara we have found sandals in almost perfect condition.

We do not know what materials were used in tanning, or indeed any of the process of dressing the skins. Almost certainly they were soaked, scraped, hammered, and polished with stone, and a one-legged stool of the First Dynasty from Sakkara may well have been used for scraping and polishing for it bears a strong resemblance to the article used for this purpose which is shown on later monuments (Fig. 135).

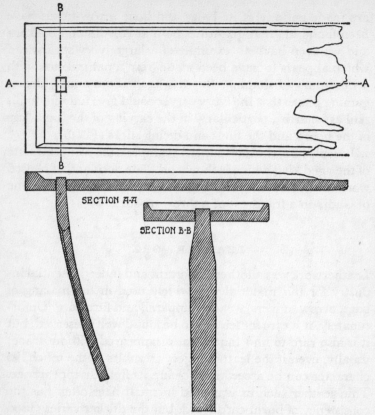

Fig. 135. One-legged stool from Sakkara

Stitching was done with leather thongs and the rectangular hole necessary for such work was made by a copper bodkin, of which many specimens have been found (Fig. 136). There is also no evidence of dyeing the leather, but arrow quivers found at Sakkara were painted with a design of blue chevrons on a yellow ground. These arrow quivers were made of stiff leather in a tubular form with a circular bottom and cross-stitching with leather thongs. Another object of leather of a similar character used for holding spears or staffs was also tubular in form, but because of its size, and to ensure rigidity, the hide was stitched round a wooden frame as shown in Fig. 137. Leather sandals, such as that shown in Fig. 138, have been found in fair preservation. The fastening straps were not attached by stitching, but were apparently socketed in the edge of the sole and held by some adhesive. Nearly all better-class chairs and

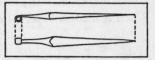

Fig. 136. Copper bodkin of the First Dynasty

beds had leather seats and mattresses, usually formed by criss-cross straps, and there is reason to suppose that cushions of soft leather were also used, although as yet certain evidence of this has not been forthcoming.

Leather thongs were also used in strengthening the joints of wooden furniture (Fig. 130).

FLINT-WORK

Although copper tools and weapons were in common use, flint was not discarded, and flint implements such as knives, scrapers, razors, hoe blades, spear- and arrow-heads, serrated sickle blades, and drill-heads continued to be manufactured throughout the period. Indeed, flint-work continued as a living industry as late as the Twelfth Dynasty.

The working of flint reached its highest perfection in the Predynastic period, but it still retained a very high standard during the First Dynasty and only began to show real deterioration towards the end of the Second Dynasty. Perhaps the finest examples of the archaic flint-worker's skill are the big knives dated to the middle of the First Dynasty which were found at Sakkara (Pl. 45).

PAPYRUS

The papyrus plant, which belongs to the sedge family, is not now found in Egypt, but in ancient times it was cultivated extensively for many purposes, the most important of which was the manufacture of writing material. It was prepared by stripping the outer rind and cutting the pith into strips which were then laid parallel, slightly overlapping each other. Then a second layer of strips was laid on top of the first at

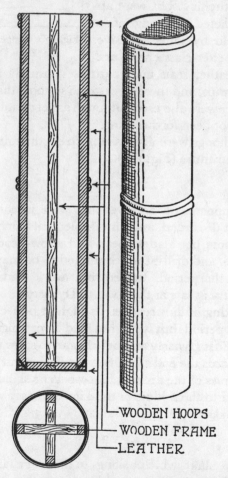

WOODEN HOOPS
WOODEN FRAME
LEATHER

Fig. 137. Cylindrical leather case from Sakkara

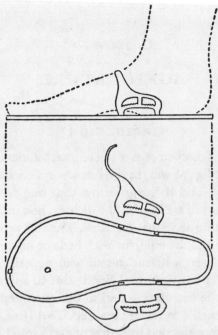

Fig. 138. Leather sandal from Sakkara

right angles. Moistened and hammered, the two layers of pith adhered together and formed one homogeneous sheet of thin writing material.

Until the recent excavations at Sakkara, there was no evidence of the existence of papyrus as a writing material, and indeed the invention of the process of its manufacture appeared unlikely at so early a period as the First Dynasty. However, two rolls of papyrus were found in a small wooden box, dated to the reign of Udimu, and although they had not been written on, there is little doubt that this was the purpose for which they had been made.

Chapter 10

AGRICULTURE

IRRIGATION

WITH all the achievements of her artists, builders, and craftsmen, archaic Egypt was, as she has always been, an agricultural country, and it is significant that one of the earliest representations of a Pharaoh shows him, hoe in hand, ceremonially cutting an irrigation canal. The rich products of her soil are the gift of the Nile, for with little or no rainfall Egypt would be a desert without the alluvial deposits brought by the great river in its annual flood. But to support a great civilization, the inundation had to be controlled so that the maximum benefits could be obtained. To do this, the areas of cultivation were divided by banks of earth into basins within which the flood waters were brought through canals. This basin irrigation system retained the water until the soil had thoroughly absorbed it and prevented its too rapid recession as the flood level sank. Thus the Nile inundated the valley and delta each July, and on the rich fertile silt left when the waters subsided in November, crops were sown, to be harvested in April and May.

We have no evidence of what method was employed in raising water to higher ground levels which, when there was a low Nile, were not reached by the flood. In later times, as today, this difficulty was overcome by the use of a primitive machine called in Arabic a *shaduf*. The *shaduf* consists of two vertical pillars between which is suspended a hinged pole with a rope and bucket at one end and a counter-weight at the other. So simple an apparatus may well have been known at this early period, for we have direct evidence that water in sufficient quantities for the cultivation of small trees was raised to the high ground in which they were planted.

PLOUGHING AND HOEING

We know little of the character of their agricultural tools, and although the plough may have been used, we have no certain evidence of its existence in archaic times. In fact the only surviving implement for breaking ground is the hoe, of which we have pictorial representations as well as actual specimens. Probably the most common form of hoe was that used by the king in Fig. 3, which was made of wood strengthened with twisted cord. But there are other implements with copper or flint blades, which, although they resemble a carpenter's adze, are by reason of their size and the lightness of the blade, probably to be identified as a form of light hoe (Fig. 139).

CEREALS

Of the cereal crops sown, we have the certain identification of emmer wheat, barley, and millet, and of fruits we have dates, sycamore figs, grapes, and *nabk* berries which are the product of the sidder tree and are rather like cherries. There is little doubt that vegetables were cultivated, but we have no knowledge of what these were. Flax for the making of textiles was obviously cultivated in considerable quantities. We know that trees were appreciated in orderly growth, and we have found the remains of unidentified shrubs planted in rows of pits on the edge of the escarpment in the archaic necropolis at Sakkara.

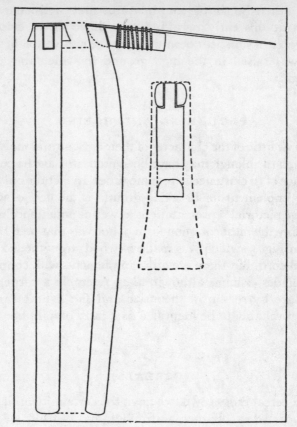

Fig. 139. Type of copper-bladed hoe

HARVESTING

For reaping, the sickle was used, and a number of very fine specimens of this agricultural implement were found in Tomb 3035 (Pl. 40). They were made of wood with a cutting edge of small serrated flint blades set in a groove and held in place by a black-coloured adhesive which has not yet been identified. After the harvest, the corn was stored in silos of which there were various types; the most common, which was transportable, was cylindrical in form and made of pottery. Built-in granaries were of two sorts: one with a cylindrical interior and the other with rows of rectangular compartments. In each type the corn was poured in through the top and withdrawn through a small door at the base (Fig. 140).

DOMESTIC ANIMALS

Apart from the cultivation of the soil, cattle-breeding was extensively practised by the archaic farmer. Judging from

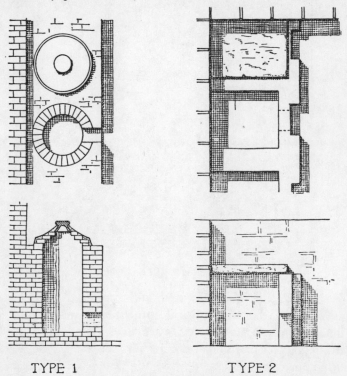

TYPE 1   TYPE 2

Fig. 140. Types of built-in granaries

the vast quantity of anatomical remains left as food offerings and from the horns from the bulls' head benches of the tombs, it would appear that their oxen belonged to that species which today is unknown in Egypt but is still bred in the Sudan. They were long-horned and of a race apparently akin to the so-called zebu.

Other domestic animals were the donkey, goat, pig, sheep, and possibly the camel.

Chapter 11

DOMESTIC LIFE

HOUSES AND FURNITURE

THE only evidence we have of the appearance of the houses of archaic Egypt comes from the tombs and coffins which, as dwellings of the dead, were obviously fair representations of those they inhabited in life. Although the circular huts of the predynastic people almost certainly survived in rural areas, and even in the poorer parts of the towns, rectangular houses with low vaulted roofs made of brick or wood were probably used by the mass of the urban population. Varying in size and quality according to the status of their owners, they were by no means primitive habitations, and indeed, judging from their tombs, the homes of the nobility must have approached almost a standard of luxury, with indoor baths and privies, separate sleeping quarters, and walls decorated with matting. This luxurious standard of living is confirmed by the existence of the comfortable household furnishings of which we have direct evidence, both from finding the actual objects in the tombs and from pictorial representations on the walls of the tomb of Hesy at Sakkara. Although this tomb was built at the beginning of the Third Dynasty, its paintings nevertheless present furniture and other objects which must have been in common use throughout the whole of the Archaic Period. Chairs and beds were made of wood embellished with wood and copper fittings, and in many cases had leather or cloth seats and mattresses fastened to the frame with leather thongs. The legs of such furniture are frequently

Fig. 141. Representations of furniture from the tomb of Hesy

carved in the form of fore and hind limbs of the bull, but simpler designs are not uncommon (see Fig. 141). This bull-leg design was greatly favoured and was used in the supports of chests, boxes, gaming-boards, and other small objects. The beds were usually low, rarely exceeding a height of 12 inches; the chairs were often no higher, so that the occupant must have rested in a more or less squatting posture. Such low chairs were perhaps used to accompany the low stone tables on which meals were served. Nevertheless, higher chairs, of what we would consider normal height, were common.

Tables, almost invariably of stone, were of two types, the commonest having a circular top and single central pedestal leg (Fig. 142) while the other has four legs and a shield-shaped top (see Fig. 143). Both types, made of alabaster or schist, are usually low and would only stand about 9 inches from the floor. With few exceptions they are small, and for eating purposes would obviously only accommodate a meal for one person. We may therefore conclude that, when feasting together, the archaic Egyptians each had their own table. High stone pedestals on which a round table top was placed were also commonly used, so that a squatting posture in eating was certainly not the invariable rule (Fig. 144). That this was so in the Second Dynasty is shown from such rare pictorial illustrations as those on the stelae recently discovered by Zaki Saad at Helwan.

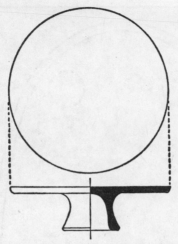

Fig. 142. Type of low round-top table

FOOD AND DRINK

With regard to the food and drink of the archaic Egyptians, we are well-informed because of the custom of leaving a meal by the side of the dead in their tombs. In a tomb of the Second Dynasty belonging to a lady of the lesser nobility at Sakkara we were fortunate in finding a complete meal, lying entirely undisturbed by the side of her coffin (Pl. 29). Such was its state of preservation that each dish was easily recognizable and the only knowledge that we lack is the order in which it was eaten. Some of the food was served on rough pottery platters and some on beautiful plates and bowls of alabaster and diorite. This gives us an indication which dish was eaten hot, because, of course, a stone vessel is useless for heating purposes. The menu of this elaborate meal was as follows (Pl. 28):

1. A form of porridge made from ground barley
2. A cooked quail, cleaned and dressed with the head tucked under the wing

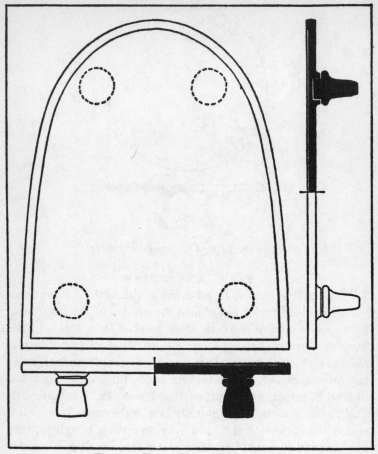

Fig. 143. Type of low shield-top table

3. Two cooked kidneys
4. A pigeon stew
5. A cooked fish, cleaned and dressed with the head removed
6. Ribs of beef
7. Small triangular loaves of bread made from emmer wheat
8. Small circular cakes
9. Stewed fruit, possibly figs

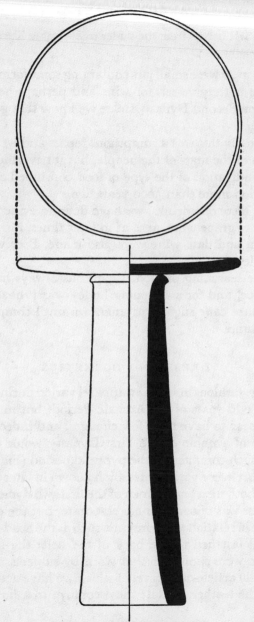

Fig. 144. High pedestal table

10. Fresh *nabk* berries from the sidder tree – rather like cherries in appearance.

With this meal were small jars containing some form of cheese and large pottery vessels for wine and perhaps beer. From pictures on Second Dynasty stelae we know that geese were also eaten.

Admittedly this was a sumptuous repast and well beyond the reach of the mass of the people, but it nevertheless gives us some indication of the type of food consumed at that remote period more than 5000 years ago.

Of the alcoholic drinks, we have definite evidence of the existence of grape wine, and, as in later times, it is probable that palm and date wine were also made. Beer was made from barley.

For the seasoning of food, Egypt has always had salt in abundance, and for sweetening honey was probably used; for of course cane sugar was unknown until comparatively modern times.

DRESS AND COSMETICS

Naturally, fashions in wearing apparel varied during the four hundred odd years of the Archaic Period, but in essentials there appear to have been few changes, and indeed the appearance of a noble of the First Dynasty would not have caused much comment in the pyramid period (Fig. 145). In fact, almost every variety of fashion known in later times was worn by both men and women of the first two dynasties. The royal dress was of course more elaborate, but the difference was more in relation to the insignia such as the head-dress and bull's tail fastened to the back of the belt; the king's kilt and tunic were similar to that worn by subjects.

The only article of apparel of which we have actual specimens is the leather sandal; these confirm to a large extent the accuracy of their depiction on such monuments as the Narmer palette (Fig. 138).

We cannot be certain if wigs were worn, as in later times, but from the limited pictorial evidence this would appear probable. Women wore their hair long, and we have found combs of wood and ivory of which the specimen bearing the

Fig. 145. Examples of male dress from the palette of Narmer

name of King Uadji is perhaps the finest example (Fig. 146). Eye paints of green, made from malachite, and dark grey, made from galena, were mixed on rectangular palettes of schist, and the beauty of the face was enhanced by the application of red powder made from haematite. Delicate sticks of ivory and wood were used in the application of cosmetics, while small vessels of alabaster, marble, schist, and crystal were used to contain unguents and other toilet liquids.

RECREATION

For indoor recreation, the favourite game was a form of draughts; but although we have found complete sets of the pieces and the board on which they were placed, we are still ignorant of the actual rules of play. There were obviously variations of the game, for we find boards marked with three or two rows of squares (Pl. 48). A complete set of 'pawns' also varies in number, some consisting of 14 pieces, 7 on each side, others consisting of 26 pieces with 13 to each player. The 'pawns', usually made of ivory or wood, all conform to two designs: a half sphere for the pieces of one side and a

Fig. 146. Comb of Uadji

cylinder tapering to a disc top for the other (Fig. 147). The presence of dice sticks with these draught sets suggests that the game was not entirely one of skill, and it would appear probable that the moves were governed by the failure or success of the 'throw' of the sticks which until late times took the place of dice (Fig. 148). Sets of gaming pieces were kept in specially fitted boxes (Fig. 149).

Another game, with moves apparently governed by the throwing of dice sticks, was played on a circular table which is marked by the image of a coiled serpent on the body of which the places are marked. The pieces, 6 in number, 3 to a side, are crouching animals, usually 3 lions and 3 lionesses, made of wood or ivory (Fig. 150). Frequently found with gaming sets of both the draughts and serpent games are small stone marbles which would appear to have been used as counters.

A series of disks of stone, copper, wood, horn, and ivory, many of them elaborately decorated, was found in the remains of a shallow wooden tray at Sakkara, and although we cannot be absolutely certain, it would appear probable that these also form part of a game. The disks, about 4 ins. in diameter, have a hole in the middle through which was a small pointed stick about 6 ins. long and from practical experiment it has been shown that a quick turn of the stick between the palms of the hands will make the disk spin in the manner of a top for a considerable period. Unfortunately, the wooden tray which contained the disks was so broken that no trace of marking remained on its floor; but we may perhaps envisage a game in which the spinning top coming to rest in a certain area would mark up a score.

In the scanty relics left to us after 5000 years, no recognizable remains of musical instruments have been found, but undoubtedly these existed. Dancing by women in unison to the clapping of hands is plainly shown on the mace-head of the 'Scorpion King' (Fig. 3).

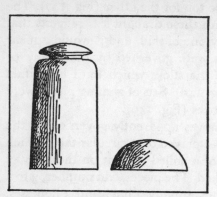

Fig. 147. Types of gaming pieces

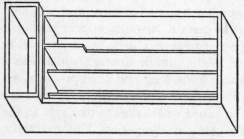

Fig. 149. Box for gaming pieces

Fig. 148. Dice-
stick of Ka'a

In outdoor sports the archaic Egyptian concentrated on hunting wild animals such as the lion, hippo, wild boar, and gazelle. His weapons of the chase were the spear, axe, mace, throwing-stick, bow and arrow, and the lasso. Although we have no pictorial evidence, we may be sure that, like his descendants of the Pyramid Age, he enjoyed fowling and fishing in the marshes.

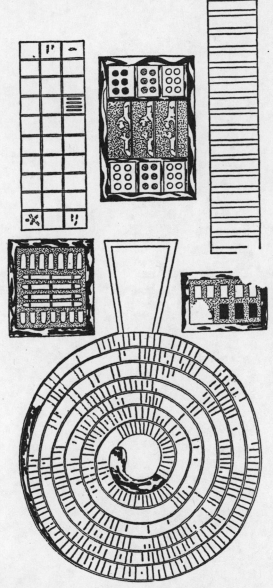

Fig. 150. Gaming sets depicted in the tomb of Hesy

Appendix

APPENDIX

Manetho's account of the First and Second Dynasties according to Africanus.

FIRST DYNASTY

1. In succession to the spirits of the Dead, the Demigods, the first royal house numbers eight kings, the first of whom Mênês of Thinis reigned for sixty-two years. He was carried off by a hippopotamus and perished.
2. Athôthis, his son, for fifty-seven years. He built the palace at Memphis; and his anatomical works are extant, for he was a physician.
3. Kenkenês, his son, for thirty-one years.
4. Uenephês, his son, for twenty-three years. In his reign a great famine seized Egypt. He erected the pyramids near Kochimi.
5. Usaphaidos, his son, for twenty years.
6. Miebidos, his son, for twenty-six years.
7. Semempsês, his son, for eighteen years. In his reign a very great calamity befell Egypt.
8. Biênechês, his son, for twenty-six years.
Total, 263 years.

SECOND DYNASTY

The Second Dynasty consists of nine kings of Thinis.
1. Boêthos, for thirty-eight years. In his reign a chasm opened at Bubastis, and many perished.
2. Kaiechôs, for thirty-nine years. In his reign the bulls, Apis at Memphis and Mnevis at Heliopolis, and the Mendesian goat were worshipped as gods.
3. Binôthris, for forty-seven years. In his reign it was decided that women might hold the kingly office.
4. Tlas, for seventeen years.
5. Sethenês, for forty-one years.
6. Chairês, for seventeen years.

7. Nephercherês, for twenty-five years. In his reign, the story goes, the Nile flowed blended with honey for eleven days.
8. Sesôchris, for forty-eight years: his stature was 5 cubits, 3 palms.
9. Chenerês, for thirty years.

Total, 302 years.

Total for the First and Second Dynasties (after the Flood) 555 years, according to the second edition of Africanus.

Bibliography

BIBLIOGRAPHY

AMÉLINEAU, E. *Les Nouvelles Fouilles d'Abydos*. Paris, 1896–1902.

BAUMGARTEL, E. *The Cultures of Prehistoric Egypt*. Oxford, 1947.

BÉNÉDITÉ, G. 'Le Couteau de Gebel el Arak.' *Monuments Piot*, XXII, 1916.

BORCHARDT, L. 'Das Grab des Menes.' *Zeitschrift für ägyptische Sprache*, XXXVI, 1938.

CAPART, J. *Primitive Art in Egypt*. London, 1905.

DARESSY, G. 'La Pierre de Palerme et la chronologie de l'ancien empire.' *Bulletin de l'Institut Français*, XII, 1916.

DERRY, D. E. 'The Dynastic Race in Egypt.' *Journal of Egyptian Archaeology*, 42, 1956.

DRIOTON, E. and VANDIER, J. *Les Peuples de l'orient méditerranéen*. Paris, 1938.

EMERY, W. B. *The Tomb of Hemaka*. Cairo, 1938.

Hor-aha. Cairo, 1939.

'A Cylinder Seal of the Uruk Period.' *Annales du Service des Antiquités de l'Égypte*, XLV, 1947.

Great Tombs of the First Dynasty, I. Cairo, 1949.

Great Tombs of the First Dynasty, II. London, 1954.

Great Tombs of the First Dynasty, III. London, 1958.

ENGELBACH, R. 'An essay on the advent of the Dynastic Race.' *Annales du Service des Antiquités de l'Égypte*, XLII, 1943.

FRANKFORT, H. *Studies in Early Pottery of the Near East*. London, 1924.

'The origin of Monumental Architecture in Egypt.' *American Journal of Semitic Languages*, LVIII, 1941.

The Birth of Civilisation in the Near East. London, 1951.

GAUTHIER, H. 'Quatre Nouveaux Fragments de la pierre de Palerme.' *Le Musée égyptien*, III, 2 fasc., 1915.

GLANVILLE, S. R. K. 'An Archaic Statuette from Abydos.' *Journal of Egyptian Archaeology*, XVII, 1931.

GRDSELOFF, B. 'Notes d'épigraphie archaïque.' *Annales du Service des Antiquites de l'Égypte*, XLIV, 1944.

HALL, H. R. *The Ancient History of the Near East*. London, 1920.

HAYES, W. C. *The Scepter of Ancient Egypt*. New York, 1953.

JUNKER, H. *Turah*. Vienna, 1913.

KANTOR, H. J. 'Further evidence of Early Mesopotamian relations with Egypt.' *Journal of Near Eastern Studies*, XI, Chicago, 1952.

LEGGE, G. F. 'The Tablets of Nagadeh and Abydos.' *Proceedings of the Society of Biblical Archaeology*, XXVIII, 1906, XXIX, 1907.

'The Titles of the Thinite Kings.' *Proceedings of the Society of Biblical Archaeology*, XXX, 1908.

MACE, A. C. *The Early Dynastic Cemeteries of Naga-ed-Der*. Part II. Leipzig, 1909.

MACRAMALLAH, R. *Un Cimetière archaïque de la classe moyenne*. Cairo, 1940.

MASSOULARD, E. *Préhistoire et protohistoire d'Égypte*. Paris, 1949.

MORGAN, J. DE. *Recherches sur les origines de l'Égypte*. Paris, 1896–7.

MURRAY, G. W. 'Early Camels in Egypt.' Extrait du *Bulletin de l'Institut Fouad Ier du Désert*, tome II. Cairo, 1952.

NEEDLER, W. 'A Flint Knife of King Djer.' *Journal of Egyptian Archaeology*, 42, 1956.

NEWBERRY, P. E. 'Menes, the founder of the Egyptian monarchy.' *Great Ones of Ancient Egypt*. London, 1929.

'The Wooden and Ivory Labels of the First Dynasty.' *Proceedings of the Society of Biblical Archaeology*, XXXIV, 1912.

'The Set Rebellion of the Second Dynasty.' *Ancient Egypt* (1922), pp. 40 ff.

NEWBERRY, P. E. and WAINWRIGHT, G. 'Udimu and the Palermo Stone.' *Ancient Egypt* (1914).

PEET, T. E. 'Antiquity of Egyptian Civilisation.' *Journal of Egyptian Archaeology*, VIII.

PETRIE, W. M. FLINDERS. *Abydos*. London, 1902–4.

Coptos. London, 1896.

Diospolis Parva. London, 1901.

A History of Egypt, vol. I. London, 1923.

Naqada and Ballas. London, 1896.

'New portions of the Annals.' *Ancient Egypt*, 1916.

Prehistoric Egypt. London, 1920.

Prehistoric Egypt Corpus. London, 1921.

The Royal Tombs of the First Dynasty. London, 1900–1.

Tarkhan. London, 1914.

Tombs of the Courtiers and *Oxyrhynkhos*. London, 1925.

PETRIE, W. M. F. and WAINWRIGHT, G. *Tarkhan I* and *Memphis V*. London, 1913.

QUIBELL, J. E. *Archaic Objects*. Cairo, 1904–5.

Archaic Mastabas. Cairo, 1923.

El Kab. London, 1898.

Hierakonpolis. London, 1900–2.

READ, M. F. W. 'Nouvelles Remarques sur la pierre de Palerme.' *Bulletin de l'Institut Français*, XII, 1916.

REISNER, G. *The Development of the Egyptian Tomb*. Oxford, 1936.
The Early Dynastic Cemeteries of Naga-ed-Der. Leipzig, 1908.

SAAD, Z. Y. *Ceiling Stelae in Second Dynasty Tombs*. Cairo, 1957.
Royal Excavations at Saqqara and Helwan. Cairo, 1948.
Royal Excavations at Helwan. Cairo, 1951.

SETHE, K. *Beiträge zur ältesten Geschichte Ägyptens*. Leipzig, 1905.

SIMPSON, W. K. 'A Statuette of King Nyneter.' *Journal of Egyptian Archaeology*, 42, 1956.

VANDIER, J. *Manuel d'archéologie égyptienne*, vol. I. Paris, 1952.

WADDELL, W. G. *Manetho*. London, 1940.

WEIGALL, A. *A History of the Pharaohs*. London, 1925.

WEILL, R. *Les Deuxième et Troisième Dynasties égyptiennes*. Paris, 1908.

Index

INDEX

FOR THE BEST IN PAPERBACKS, LOOK FOR THE

In every corner of the world, on every subject under the sun, Penguin represents quality and variety – the very best in publishing today.

For complete information about books available from Penguin – including Puffins, Penguin Classics and Arkana – and how to order them, write to us at the appropriate address below. Please note that for copyright reasons the selection of books varies from country to country.

In the United Kingdom: Please write to *Dept E.P., Penguin Books Ltd, Harmondsworth, Middlesex, UB7 0DA.*

If you have any difficulty in obtaining a title, please send your order with the correct money, plus ten per cent for postage and packaging, to *PO Box No 11, West Drayton, Middlesex*

In the United States: Please write to *Dept BA, Penguin, 299 Murray Hill Parkway, East Rutherford, New Jersey 07073*

In Canada: Please write to *Penguin Books Canada Ltd, 2801 John Street, Markham, Ontario L3R 1B4*

In Australia: Please write to the *Marketing Department, Penguin Books Australia Ltd, P.O. Box 257, Ringwood, Victoria 3134*

In New Zealand: Please write to the *Marketing Department, Penguin Books (NZ) Ltd, Private Bag, Takapuna, Auckland 9*

In India: Please write to *Penguin Overseas Ltd, 706 Eros Apartments, 56 Nehru Place, New Delhi, 110019*

In the Netherlands: Please write to *Penguin Books Netherlands B.V., Postbus 195, NL–1380AD Weesp*

In West Germany: Please write to *Penguin Books Ltd, Friedrichstrasse 10–12, D–6000 Frankfurt/Main 1*

In Spain: Please write to *Alhambra Longman S.A., Fernandez de la Hoz 9, E–28010 Madrid*

In Italy: Please write to *Penguin Italia s.r.l., Via Como 4, I-20096 Pioltello (Milano)*

In France: Please write to *Penguin Books Ltd, 39 Rue de Montmorency, F-75003 Paris*

In Japan: Please write to *Longman Penguin Japan Co Ltd, Yamaguchi Building, 2–12–9 Kanda Jimbocho, Chiyoda-Ku, Tokyo 101*